Clinical Guidelines for Assessment and Treatment

Of Older Adults with ADD

By

Robert W. Hiester, Psy.D.

And

George Lawrence, Ed. D.

INFINITY PUBLISHING

ISBN 978-0-7414-0949-2

Published February 2002

INFINITY PUBLISHING
1094 New DeHaven Street, Suite 100
West Conshohocken, PA 19428-2713
Toll-free (877) BUY BOOK
Local Phone (610) 941-9999
Fax (610) 941-9959
Info@buybooksontheweb.com
www.buybooksontheweb.com

Abstract

When older adults seek treatment for depression, anxiety, or other conditions such as obsessive/compulsive behavior and substance abuse, health care professionals frequently fail to consider the possible diagnosis of Attention Deficit Disorder. Usually their symptoms are attributed to the problems of aging such as stress from losses, retirement, and memory decline. For many years ADD was thought to be only a childhood disorder. We now know that between 25 to 35 percent of children diagnosed with ADD will continue having the disorder into adulthood. It was only during this last decade that adults were recognized as having ADD and few if any research studies have been done regarding ADD in older adults. Receiving the proper diagnosis and treatment can help those over 55 who have ADD significantly.

This guide describes assessment methods and treatment modalities, which can be used for older adults by non-gerontologically trained professionals. Techniques for differentiating between other disorders and ADD are included in this guide. Unique characteristics presented by older adults with ADD are discussed and compared to younger adults with ADD. Coping skills, which often mask the symptoms making assessment very difficult, are addressed and treatment methods applicable to older adults with ADD are presented in this guide. Additional sources of information on ADD and support groups are presented in the appendices.

Table of Contents

Preface

The idea for this clinical handbook on ADD in older adults (55 years and older) came from the experiences of two psychologists, both in their 60's, and both with a professional interest in adult ADD. One found in his practice those older adults, never before diagnosed with ADD, were dealing with symptoms and experiences of ADD. The other discovered that ADD described his own behavior and experiences, and those of an adult son, once he began to closely study ADD.

Robert not only studied ADD extensively and diagnosed and treated clients, but also has lived with ADD personally, undiagnosed until he was in his mid sixties. In addition, he has a son who at age five, in 1959, was sent home from school because he was too disruptive. Unfortunately, Robert was not aware of ADD at that time despite the fact that he had studied psychology in college. Their family physician prescribed Phenobarbital to quiet his son down. Robert developed many coping skills to compensate for his ADD but continued to have many of the symptoms. As an adult Robert's son has chosen to use his coping skills to function and does not want psychopharmacologic treatment.

Since a psychiatrist prescribed Ritalin Robert's ADD symptoms been have greatly reduced and he has found the results from taking the medication both helpful and healing. Robert had developed many coping skills and has been very successful professionally partly because of having the condition however; relationship issues and attention issues have caused many frustrating problems for him. Many of the techniques presented in this guide Robert developed on his own out of need are the same as those recommended by numerous experts in the field.

A search of the literature yielded virtually no information that considered both geriatrics and ADD. The developmental issues of aging through the sixth decade of life and beyond, and the lack of early awareness of ADD as a significant and frequently lasting condition, each present unique challenges to both older adults who have lived with ADD all of their lives and to the practitioners who may treat them or consult with their families. Some come as clients for a variety of reasons, but seldom for the symptoms of ADD alone at this time of life. Some are discovered during the diagnosis of a younger family member, a grandchild, or a younger adult son or daughter. Since ADD was not a well known condition until they were well into their adult years, today's older adults with ADD have learned to cope with their symptoms, to varying degrees, or have lived with low self-esteem and labels like "spacey," "unreliable," "ineffective," or "always irritable."

This handbook is meant to be a first effort to provide practitioners some tools for helping these individuals for whom diagnosis and treatment can help improve their lives.

It is our hope that this handbook will be helpful in the practices of:

1. Mental health and medical practitioners working with older adults in a general practice
2. Geriatric practitioners without familiarity with ADD
3. ADD practitioners without geriatric familiarity

George Lawrance, Ed.D.

Acknowledgements

I want to thank the mentors and employees of North Central University for the wonderful education I received in the PsyD program. While taking a course in ADHD at NCU I realized that I have the disorder and for that reason chose to specialize in counseling individuals with the disorder and writing about the disorder. I was allowed by the university to write this book as my project for my PsyD.

I especially want to thank my mentor on this project, Dr. Richard Jones. His excellent suggestions certainly improved the quality of my book.

I want to thank my wife Barb for putting up with me during this time-consuming process and for transcribing much of the manuscript on our word processor. Also, special thanks to Phyllis Sloan for her encouragement, support and editing. George Lawrence, and Doris Vinnedge for proofreading my manuscript.

I also want to thank the numerous authors whose work contributed to the knowledge which, made this book possible.

Introduction

When older adults seek treatment for depression, anxiety, or other conditions such as obsessive/compulsive behavior, and substance abuse, health care professionals frequently fail to consider the possible diagnosis of Attention Deficit Disorder. Often their presenting symptoms are attributed to the problems of aging such as stress from losses, retirement, and memory decline. These same symptoms may also result from ADD, a lifelong condition.

As our population age's clinicians will be asked to diagnose and treat an increasing number of older adults. Many of these clinicians have little or no specialized training in geriatrics or gerontology (Scogin, F. and Prohaska, M., 1993). One of the most common problems expressed by older adults is memory decline and poor memory frequently a common symptom of individuals who have ADD. Poor memory in an older adult may have been a lifelong problem caused by ADD rather than the aging process, which could have been treated when they were younger and can be treated very effectively at this stage of their life cycle.

Many clinicians are unaware that a significant number of older adults have ADD, which could not have been diagnosed and treated when they were of school age in 1950 or earlier when information about ADD was not generally available to health care professionals and educators.

It has been only very recently that ADD was recognized as a disorder that in many cases continues through the entire life cycle. It was during the late 1980's that mental health professionals began to understand that ADD continues beyond the adolescent years (NIH, 1998). Even today many professionals do not understand that ADD exists in adults (Jackson and Farrugia, 1997) let alone in older adults. Hence their presenting characteristics are often diagnosed as other conditions.

ADD, however, is present in an estimated 2 to 7 percent of the adult population, which represents 2 to 5 million people (Khouzam, Hanrig, R., 1997). Recent surveys show that 30 to 50 percent of children with ADD will continue to have symptoms in adulthood (Barkley, 1990).

The purpose of this guide is to help the non-gerontologtically trained professionals understand how to assess the difference between normal aging processes and ADD as the cause for certain presenting symptoms. Also, this guide will cover possible coexisting disorders that some older adults with ADD may have. It is not the purpose of this guide to address the diagnosis and treatment of other disorders, nor to cover clients in other life cycle stages. Only older adults (those over 55) will be addressed.

There has been very little information until recently on adult ADD and few articles about ADD mention older adults other than as anecdotal information. Roy-Berne, et al. (1997) included some adults up to the age of 64 in their diagnostic study of adult ADD, but they presented no findings specific to their participants 55 and older. Biederman (1998) describes the case history of a 55-year-old man recently diagnosed with ADD after the diagnosis of ADD was given to his twin sons. No articles have been found that relates the life issues of older adults to ADD.

This guide begins by briefly defining what ADD is and what causes it, then addresses issues that are specific to the older adult population having ADD.

Differential diagnosis and treatment modalities are presented. Self-help techniques will be given as well as suggestions for addressing family issues arising from the disorder. In the appendices sources of more information and self-help are given.

CHAPTER 1

What is ADD

Attention deficit disorder (ADD) is a neurobiological syndrome, involving in-attention, impulsivity, and sometimes hyperactivity. These problems are developmentally inappropriate and affect many aspects of a person's life. ADD is one of the most common psychiatric disorders of childhood and adolescence. Recent clinical experience and research has documented the continuation of the disorder into adulthood (Williams and Wilkins, 1997). Far more is known about the disorder in children and adolescents than in adults. Until recently professionals considered ADD to be a childhood disturbance in which symptoms of distractibility, decreased impulse control, insecurity, and restlessness dissipated during adolescence and seemed no longer evident in adulthood. Although this pattern does hold for more than half of ADD children there is increasing evidence that some ADD children continue to have many of the symptoms of ADD as adults (Wender, 1987).

It is believed the syndrome we now call ADD has been with us for centuries. It was considered "bad behaviors" earlier in human existence. Credit for its first being defined as a syndrome goes to a British pediatrician George Frederic Still. In a series of lectures to the Royal College of Physicians in 1902 he described some children he saw in his practice who were difficult to control, showing signs of "lawlessness," lacking "inhibitory volition," and in general being obstreperous, dishonest, and willful. He hypothesized that the cause was biologically inherited or due to injury at birth rather than bad parenting or mood turpitude (Hallowell, 1994). Since that time the disorder has been referred to by different names including minimal brain dysfunction (MBD), hyper kinetic reaction of childhood, and attention deficit disorder (ADD). DSM-III (Diagnostic and Statistical Manual of Mental Disorders) had two classifications: ADD-H (hyperactivity), and ADD-R (Attention Deficit Disorder Residual Type).

In 1960 Stella Class wrote about "hyperactivity child syndrome." She saw the symptoms as part of a "physiologic hyperactivity" whose causes were biological rather than environmentally induced (Hallowell, 1994).

In the 1970's researchers identified major traits, which included:

1. Hyperactivity
2. Impulsivity
3. Difficulty regulating arousal
4. Need for immediate gratification

Since the 1980's a great deal of research has been done on children and adolescent who have ADD. Researchers have evaluated adult clients with significant symptoms of ADD not diagnosed in childhood. It is felt that the reason for the lack of adult diagnoses of ADD is because the adults present atypical symptoms or have learned to cope with some of their symptoms (Jackson and Farrugia, 1997).

Recent longitudinal studies have provided significant evidence that ADD can be a chronically disabling condition. Researchers have reported continued impairment as children diagnosed with ADD age into adulthood (Barkley, Fisher, Edelbrock, Smallish, 1990).

ADD was thought to be a disorder of hyperactivity, which affected primarily male children who outgrew it as they became teenagers. It is now recognized that ADD affects millions of girls and women and may or may not include hyperactivity.

Please note that the abbreviation ADD is used throughout this guide rather than AD/HD since hyperactivity is not always part of the disorder. The Diagnostic Statistical Manual Fourth Edition (DSM-IV) recognizes it as having two distinct subtypes, with and without hyperactivity. ADD in the DSM-IV will be discussed in the chapter on diagnosis. Daniel Amen (1997), a psychiatrist, has identified five subtypes of ADD. These are:

1. ADD with hyperactivity
2. ADD without hyperactivity
3. ADD over focused
4. ADD limbic
5. ADD temporal lobe

Note: these may occur in various combinations, which will be discussed later in this guide.

Often adults with mental health difficulties are thought to have discrete disorders, but a history of ADD is more than a coincidental factor in adult psychiatric problems. A systematic search of the psychiatric and psychological literature for co-morbidity of ADD in adults was conducted. The researchers found that there is considerable co-morbidity of ADD with conduct disorder, mood disorders, anxiety disorders and learning disabilities (Biederman, Newcorn, and Sprich, 1991).

It is even more difficult to identify ADD in older adults due to the similarity of symptoms with the aging process. Individuals with ADD have poor memories, which can be mistaken for dementia in older adults. This will be discussed in more detail in the diagnosis chapter.

There has been so much controversy over whether ADD is a disorder that the National Institute of Health professionals conducted a survey to determine if consensus existed on ADD being a disorder. They concluded, "Although an independent diagnostic test for ADD does not exist, there is evidence supporting the validity of the disorder. Further research is needed on the dimensional aspects of ADD, as well as the co-morbid (coexisting) conditions present in both childhood and adult forms" (NIH, 1999).

Despite the large amount of research being conducted during the last decade and progress in assessment, diagnosis, and treatment of ADD, there remains a great deal of controversial information. The major concern comes from uninformed public sectors, in reaction to the use of psycho stimulants for both short-term and long-term treatments. These medications have been used successfully for over 30 years to reduce the symptoms of ADD with few if any side effects and no contra-indications from their long-term use. However, scientific studies needed to demonstrate their safety, including family studies, epidemiological studies and long-term studies, have not been sufficient. Significant controversy remains in regard to the use of stimulants even in the professional area (Goldman, Genel, Bezman, and Slanetz, 1998). More discussions of stimulant medications are included in the treatment modality chapter.

Like most mental health disorders ADD diagnostic criteria involve patient history and behavioral assessment without the availability of laboratory or radiological confirmation. It has an early onset and extensive course, often requiring treatment over the entire life span, and treatment often includes stimulant medications that have abuse or diversion potential.

The majority of adults and older adults experience the same symptoms as children. Stress intolerance is also common, which leads to anger. Older adults presenting these characteristics are frequently misdiagnosed as having some other disorder. A significant number of older adults are high consumers of alcohol. Clinicians assume the alcohol consumption to be the cause of their difficulties, when it is more a means of self-medication by the client to reduce his or her symptoms. Alcohol addiction and ADD will be discussed in a later chapter in this guide.

Recent research with brain wave imaging has potential for validation of ADD assessment. This will be covered in the chapter discussing causes of ADD. At this time most professionals feel that more investigation needs to be done before this can be accepted as an assessment tool. However, it is well along the way toward becoming part of the assessment and diagnostic process.

Since older adults will seek help from adult oriented clinicians without child specialty training, there is a need for assessment guidelines based on the disorder as it presents for older adults. Clinicians who work with older adults need to become aware that ADD often continues throughout the entire life span. There are likely to be millions of older adults suffering from ADD since researchers now believe 30-50 % of children who suffer from ADD will continue to have the symptoms through their entire life span. Recent studies have shown that ADD in adulthood does indicate continued or increased impairment (Jackson and Farrugia, 1997).

Many adults and likely few if any older adults with ADD were properly diagnosed as children because the presenting symptoms of ADD were not understood until recently, and only very recently considered to be a lifetime disorder.

When today's older adults were children, ADD was not widely known to be a disorder caused by biological circumstances prior to or during birth, and therefore most adults with ADD were not properly diagnosed as children. Because of this, they grew up struggling with a neurobiological disability they did not know they had. Some were told they were "hyper-kinetic" or "hyperactive" and they would outgrow the symptoms. Still others were thought to be troublesome children. Many older adults developed other problems because of their ADD, which in turn masked their ADD symptoms.

Some adults with ADD who are restless, easily distracted, have difficulty sustaining attention, are impulsive and impatient, have frequent mood swings or have difficulty planning ahead, can be misidentified as suffering from depression, bipolar, and other disorders. It is unfortunate that no research has been done specifically related to older adults who have ADD. Increasingly, there are studies of younger adults, but many of the issues facing older adults are different and need to be recognized so that assessment, diagnosis, and treatment can be used to reduce their symptoms.

In later chapters of this guide methods to rule out other disorders for older adults will be presented. Most importantly will be methods to recognize ADD in older adults and prevent misdiagnosis.

It is also important for the clinician to realize that older adults have no idea that ADD is an adult disorder and certainly not an older adult disorder. Many older adults with ADD can be helped significantly to improve their quality of life.

CHAPTER 2

What Causes ADD

Scientists have developed many theories about what causes ADD. An early theory was that minor head injuries or undetectable damage to the brain, possibly occurring at birth, caused ADD. For this reason the disorder was called "minimal brain damage" or "minimal brain dysfunction" for many years.

Head injuries can cause ADD; however, this explains only a small number of cases. Other theories were suggested, such as refined sugar and food additives as causes of hyperactivity in children. The National Institutes of Health studied the food additive issue and concluded that restricted diet only seemed to help about 5% of children with ADD, mostly young children. In 1998 NIH concluded that ADD is not usually caused by:

- Too much TV
- Food allergies
- Excess sugar
- Poor home life
- Poor schools

Genetics is now believed to be a significant cause of ADD. Studies of twins have shown that in 70 to 90% of twin pairs where one has the disorder, both twins will have ADD. Identical twins have a much higher risk than non-identical twins, since identical twins have essentially the same genetic material while non-identical twins do not (Sudderth and Kandel, 1997). If a child has the disorder there is a 15-20% risk that one or both parents will have the disorder. If a parent has the disorder there is 25-54% risk that one or more of their children will have the disorder. Several research teams have been looking for genes related to ADD, two have been found so far.

Research has found that the following are the best-established causes at this time (Amen, 1997):

- High genetic transmission, involving the genes for the neurotransmitter Dopamine
- Maternal alcohol or drug use during pregnancy
- Birth problems (lack of oxygen at birth, jaundice, etc)
- Head trauma: sometimes even minor ones can affect learning and behavior
- Radiation exposure (very rare)
- Meningitis/encephalitis as a preschooler
- High fevers for more than 24 hours
- Other risk factors (Nathan, Groman, and Salkind, 1999) such as infection during the first trimester of pregnancy, over-stimulating environment during infancy or early childhood.

The mechanism is thought to stem from neurotransmitter dysfunction (dopamine/or epinephrine) and decreased frontal lobe cerebral blood flow.

The brain constantly sends electrical impulses back and forth through chemicals called neurotransmitters. Minor damage or insufficient development to a specific area of the brain such as the frontal lobe might cause ADD. Also, lower amounts of biochemical might affect transmission rates. These neurotransmitters are the chemical messengers released from the nerve endings, which significantly affect human behavior. The frontal lobes of the brain are large and affect behaviors such as sequencing, drive, and executive control. This area is unique to human beings (Sudderth and Kandel, 1997).

Executive control is related to social appropriateness. Loss of executive control leads to behaviors that are not socially appropriate such as blurting out comments, impulsivity, distractibility, and difficulty completing tasks. Recently new tools and techniques for studying the brain have been developed which has resulted in more theories about the functional causes of ADD.

How the brain's anatomic system works is being studied by using neuroimaging techniques such as positron emission tomography (PET) and single photon emission computer tomography (SPECT) scans. This is allowing researchers to study differences in brain metabolism and activity between individuals who have ADD and symptom free individuals. Also, effects from medications such as stimulants have been studied and found to change brain activity to a more normal condition (NIH, 1998).

The National Institute for Mental Health used advanced brain imaging techniques to compare brain metabolism between adults with ADD and adults without ADD. They found reduced metabolism in those participants with ADD. Brain scan images produced by positron emission tomography (PET) show differences between adults with ADD and those who are symptom-free (NIH,1998).

There is an increasing amount of evidence pointing to the frontal lobe impairment as the primary area of malfunction in ADD. The emotion-laden information is relayed from other parts of the brain to the frontal lobes. This allows present experience to be integrated with past experience stored in memory before reaction takes place. This is the executive function of the frontal lobe. Through the integration process, impulsive emotional responses are presented and compared to past experience to prevent inappropriate behavior. If the frontal lobes fail, there is impairment of attention and impulse modulation (Sudderth and Kandel, 1997).

Glucose is the primary source of energy for the brain. Scientists at the NIMH used a PET (positron emission tomography) scanner to measure the level of glucose used in the frontal areas of the brain that control attention and inhibit impulses. They found that by examining a patient's level of glucose brain activity could be observed. As local activity in the brain increases, the amount of glucose used also increases (Sudderth and Kandel, 1997).

PET scans of adults with a history of ADD who have at least one child with ADD were compared with adults who were symptom-free. Adults with ADD used less glucose in the frontal lobe area compared to adults who were symptom-free (NIMH, 1999).

Studies show 8-15% less brain volume in individuals with ADD in the orbital, stratum, and cerebellum regions of the brain. These regions are interconnected and inhibit motor responses, affecting an individual's inhibitions and reaction. The smaller regions appear more in the right hemisphere. The observed differences in this study were not the result of injury (Pardo, Fox, and Raichle, 1991). Researchers' Sandson, Bachna and Morin (2000), who examined 58 adults who were diagnosed as having ADD, corroborated this earlier finding.

Researchers used neuroimaging to examine S–ADHD (Secondary Attention Deficit Hyperactivity Disorder) in children from 4-19 who suffered severe and moderate closed head injury. Results of their study supported the association between S-ADHD and injury in either the thalamus or basal ganglia or both. This supported the theory that a frontal-thalamic-brain stem circuit plays a major role in disorders of attention (Gerring, Brady, Chen, Quinn, Herskovits, Bandeen-Roche, Denckla, and Bryan (2000).

Joel Lubar found that children and teenagers with ADD have different electrical brain wave patterns than control groups. Concentration attempts by children and adolescents with ADD increased the amount of slow brain wave activity in their frontal lobes rather than the usual increase in fast brain wave activity seen in the control group. When medication reduces symptoms there is a normalization of brain waves (Amen, 1997).

Daniel Amen (1997) using SPECT imaging also found that the more individuals with ADD try to concentrate, the worse their concentration gets. He found that the prefrontal lobe activity reduced during a concentration task compared to a resting state of activity for individuals with ADD.

A significant amount of progress has been made in investigating the causes of ADD, but more research is needed before a final conclusion can be reached.

CHAPTER 3

Diagnosing ADD in Older Adults

This chapter presents the criteria and some tools for diagnosing adult ADD. It also addresses the issues particular to older adults and ADD. The clinician will find an emphasis on interviewing for pertinent history from childhood to the present as well as current functioning. Differential diagnosis will be covered in the next chapter.

Diagnosing ADD in older adults is complicated by several factors:

1. Diagnostic criteria were designed for young children and have not been adjusted for older adults.
2. Older adults often have disorders that present symptoms similar to those of ADD.
3. Often older adults with ADD will be diagnosed as having some other disorder such as dementia, depression, or anxiety, which masks their actual disorder, since many mental health professionals who diagnose and treat older adults have no training or experience with ADD. Only recently was ADD found to be an adult disorder. There is virtually no research on older adult ADD.
4. Older adults with ADD are not aware the disorder can exist through the entire life cycle.
5. Older adults have developed many coping skills to deal with their disorder.

While some professionals question ADD as a legitimate disorder (Breggin, 1998), the National Institute of Health found that there is validity in the diagnosis of ADD as a disorder with broadly accepted symptoms and behavioral characteristics that define the disorder (NIH Census Statement, 1998).

The DSM-IV (1994) contains clear diagnostic criteria for AD/HD (ADD); however, there are several areas of difficulty. An older adult's ADD symptoms may not meet the DSM-IV criteria due to a lack of confirmable childhood history. Frequently there is complicating psychiatric or substance abuse co-morbidity. Older adults often have no living relative who can recall their childhood and they may have difficulty remembering their history before age seven. Several techniques will be presented later in this chapter to assist them in recall of their behavior before age seven.

Alcohol abuse is common in older adults for self-medicating, which makes it more difficult to assess and diagnose ADD. In addition, the use of marijuana may cause a person to appear to have ADD (Amen, 1997). This issue will be addressed in the chapter on differential diagnosis. A large degree of psychiatric co-morbidity may exist, which makes it hard to know what conditions are causing the symptoms (Roy-Byrne, Scheele, Brinkley, Ward, Wiatrak, Russo, Townes, Varley, 1997). Depression can be caused by ADD and often is, which makes it very difficult to determine whether it is an ADD symptom of the inattention type or clinical depression. ADD can also cause anxiety. Bi-polar disorder and ADD have many common symptoms such as poor concentration and distractibility. Forgetfulness is common to ADD, depression, and dementia.

These are examples of issues that make it very difficult for the clinicians to arrive at a valid assessment. There are few scales or measures used by mental health professionals to assess and document the adult client's level of ADD dysfunction. It is not clear how much impairment is clinically significant and there is a challenging gray area between ADD and non-ADD (Roy-Byrne et al. 1997). As stated earlier, DSM-IV requires childhood history and older adults most often do not have many older living relatives. They may not have report cards or other historical information, which would aid them in recall of their childhood history before age 7. Also, many older adults suffer from failing memory. Academic history may still offer good information since many older adults with ADD have learned to cope with their disorder, have later improved their performance, and earned advanced degrees in some cases.

The first task for the health care professional is to gather information that rules out other causes for the individual's behavior. This initial assessment must include an extensive interview, an accurate history, and an evaluation of the client's behavioral and functional performances. A number of other psychiatric, medical, and neurologic disorders such as traumatic brain injury, epilepsy and depression can cause disturbances such as inattention and/or activity level (Goldman, Genel, Bezman, and Slanetz, 1998).

In Practice Parameters for the Assessment and Treatment of Children, Adolescents, and Adults with Attention-Deficit/Hyperactivity Disorder (Williams and Wilkins, 1997) the following assessment procedure was recommended:

ADULT ASSESSMENT

A complete psychiatric assessment is indicated; see American Psychiatric Association Work Group on Psychiatric Evaluation of Adults (1995).

A. Interview with patient.
  1. Developmental history.
  2. Present and past DSM-IV symptoms of ADHD (may use symptom or criterion checklist or self-report form).
  3. History of development and context of symptoms and resulting past and present impairment.
    a. School (learning, academic productivity, and behavior).
    b. Work.
    c. Family.
    d. Peers.
  4. History of other psychiatric disorders.
  5. History of psychiatric treatment.
  6. DSM-IV symptoms of possible alternate or comorbid psychiatric diagnoses, specially:
    a. Personality disorder

b. Mood disorders – depression or mania
c. Anxiety disorders
d. Dissociative disorder
e. Tic disorder (including Tourette's disorder)
f. Substance use disorder
g. Learning disorders

7. Strengths (e.g., talents and abilities).
8. Mental status examination.

B. Standardized rating scales completed by the patient's parent.

C. Medical history.

1. Medical or neurological primary diagnosis (e.g., thyroid disease, seizure disorder, migraine, head trauma).
2. Medications that could be causing symptoms (e.g., phenobarbital, antihistamines, theophylline, sympathomimetics, steroids).

D. Family history.

1. ADHD, tic disorders, substance use disorders, CD, personality disorders, mood disorders, anxiety disorders.
2. Developmental and learning disorders.
3. Family coping style, level of organization, and resources.
4. Family stressors
5. Abuse or neglect (as victim or perpetrator).

E. Interview with significant other or parent, if available.

F. Physical evaluation. (including hearing loss evaluation)

1. Examination within 12 months or less if clinical condition has changed.
2. Further medical or neurological evaluation as indicated.

G. School information.

1. Standardized rating scales if completed during childhood.

2. Narrative childhood reports regarding learning, academic productivity, and behavior.
3. Reports of testing (e.g., standardized group achievement tests and individual evaluations).
4. Grades and attendance records.

H. Referral for additional evaluations if indicated.
   1. Psycho educational evaluation.
      a. IQ.
      b. Academic achievement.
      c. Learning disorders evaluation.
   2. Neuropsychological testing.
   3. Vocational evaluation.

TYPICAL PRESENTING COMPLAINTS FOR OLDER ADULTS WITH ADD ARE (AMEN, 1997):

1. Concerns about child or grandchild with ADD after health care professionals asked for a family history.
2. Poor work performance.
   a. Deficient sustained attention to reading and other activities.
   b. Easily bored by tedious material
   c. Poor organization and planning
   d. Procrastination
   e. Restlessness
   f. Impulsive decision making
   g. Cannot work well independently
   h. Does not listen carefully to directions
   i. Frequent impulsive job changes
   j. Poor academic grades for ability
   k. Often late for work/appointments
   l. Frequently misplaces things
   m. Trouble thinking clearly
   n. Generally poor self-discipline
3. Moodiness
4. Chronic anxiety

5. Substance abuse
6. Uncontrolled anger at their children and grandchildren
7. Marital problems
8. Sleep problems
9. Financial problems
10. Impulsiveness

Note: For older adults it is very important to establish that these have been lifetime occurrences. Many of these symptoms could be construed as aging problems, which means the counselor needs to use extreme care not to rule out ADD without a through assessment.

For older adults, having ADD under-diagnosed or misdiagnosed can lead to low self-esteem, frustration and vocational failure. As adults prior to retirement they may have had career difficulties, loss of jobs and relationship difficulties.

Since older adults have difficulty recalling childhood symptoms, having parents or siblings available may yield more accurate information. During the initial assessment the following questions might help establish older adult ADD (Khouzam, 1997):

1. Do you seem to listen when spoken to directly?
2. Do people often have to repeat what they say to you? (presuming no significant hearing loss)
3. Is it difficult for you to finish tasks, even when you know how to perform them?
4. Is (was) it difficult for you to plan and organize your work assignments?
5. Is it difficult for you to wait in line?
6. Is it difficult for you to sit still? Do you frequently get out of your seat even when you are supposed to remain seated?

The initial step of the assessment process is the first interview, which covers both childhood and adult behavior. The clinical interview is the most effective method used to identify ADD with an older adult client. It is crucial to identify symptoms and behavior during childhood since ADD has an early onset. Detailed memories of childhood behavior can be particularly difficult for an older adult. The counselor must rely on self-descriptions from the client and more global descriptions from family and friends. It is useful to use open-ended questions about childhood behavior and school performance such as finishing assignments and other difficulties. If the client has any school records or class pictures these would be helpful to aid in recall. Questions about relationship difficulties, behavior difficulties and quality of self-esteem and the basis for it will help the counselor assess possible ADD in the older adult. Open-ended questions about current behaviors are very helpful to aid the older adult client to remember behavioral characteristics. Areas to question include coping with stress, family of origin and acquired family relationship problems; i.e., forgetfulness, time management, difficulty with task management, and organizing such as desk, workbench, and storage.

Boys with AD/HD combined or predominantly hyperactive-impulsive type are often identified early in life, which causes them to stand out from others. AD/HD predominantly inattentive type girls, on the other hand, often are ignored because they are labeled as "social butterflies" (Amen, 1997).

During the interview it is important for the clinician to observe the client's behavior. Clues such as impulsivity in responding, interrupting, distractibility, hyperactivity, and short attention span should be considered.

First interview components:

1. Family history
2. Pregnancy and birth history
3. Medical and physical factors
4. Developmental history
5. School history
6. Home history
7. College and other educational experience
8. Job history
9. Inter personal history

Head injury, as part of the birth history should be considered. Also, secondary ADD can result from childhood head injury (Peter Roy-Byrne et al. 1997). Impulsivity and inattention can lead to more frequent traffic violations.

It is very helpful to have a "significant other" present for the assessment portion of the interview. This may be a spouse, parent, or friend.

ASSESSMENT REPORT

A typical assessment report of an Adult with ADD contains (Weiss, 1997):

Presenting Problems
School History
Family History
Personal Life
Physical History
Addiction History
Job and Career History
Behavioral History
Significant Other Interview
Observation
Summary

The diagnosis of ADD in older adults has not yet been defined beyond the criteria for younger adults. As discussed earlier it is a very complex process. Diagnosis involves identifying ADD symptoms and ruling out alternative conditions, which could manifest themselves in similar ways. If no other medical or psychiatric explanation can explain the client's behavior, the clinician can be reasonably sure the client has ADD and provide treatment for that condition.

CRITERIA FOR AD/HD from DSM-IV
Attention-Deficit/Hyperactivity Disorder

A. Meeting the criteria for either (1) or (2) is necessary to make the diagnosis.

(1) six (or more) of the following symptoms of inattention have persisted for at least six months to a degree that is maladaptive and inconsistent with developmental level:

Inattention

(a) ____ often fails to give close attention to details or makes careless mistakes in schoolwork, work, or other activities

(b) ____ often has difficulty sustaining attention in tasks or play activities

(c) ____ often does not seem to listen when spoken to directly

(d) ____ often does not follow through on instructions and fails to finish schoolwork, chores, or duties in the workplace (not due to oppositional behavior or failure to understand instructions)

(e) ____ often has difficulty organizing tasks and activities

(f) ____ often avoids, dislikes, or is reluctant to engage in tasks that require sustained mental effort (such as schoolwork or homework)

(g) ____ often loses things necessary for tasks or activities (e.g., toys, school assignments, pencils, books, or tools)

(h) ____ is often easily distracted by extraneous stimuli

(i) ____ is often forgetful in daily activities

(1) six (or more) of the following symptoms of hyperactivity-impulsivity have persisted for at least six months to a degree that is maladaptive and inconsistent with developmental level:

Hyperactivity

(a) ____ often fidgets with hands or feet or squirms in seat

(b) ____ often leaves seat in classroom or in other situations in which remaining seated is expected

(c) ____ often runs about or climbs excessively in situations in which it is inappropriate (in adolescents or adults, may be limited to subjective feelings of restlessness)

(d) ____ often has difficulty playing or engaging in leisure activities quietly

(e) ____ is often "on the go" or often acts as if "driven by a motor"

(f) ____ often talks excessively

Impulsivity

(g) ____ often blurts out answers before questions have been completed

(h) ____ often has difficulty awaiting turn

(i) ____ often interrupts or intrudes on others (e.g., interrupts conversations or games)

B. The onset of at least some symptoms must be before age seven and they must have lasted at least for six months
C. Some impairment from the symptoms is present in two or more settings (e.g., school [or work] and at home)
D. There must also be clear evidence of clinically significant impairment in social, academic, or occupational functioning
E. The symptoms do not occur exclusively during the course of a Pervasive Developmental Disorder, Schizophrenia, or other Psychotic Disorder and are not accounted for by another mental disorder (e.g., mood disorder, anxiety disorder, dissociative disorder, or a personality disorder)

Based on DSM-IV criteria, there can be three subtypes:
314.01 AD/HD, combined type,
If both criterion for 1 and 2 are met

314.00 AD/HD, predominantly inattentive type,
If criterion 1 is met but criterion 2 is not

314.01 AD/HD, predominantly hyperactive-impulsive type,
If criterion 2 is met but criterion 1 is not

Amen (1997) lists the following sub-types:

ADD without Hyperactivity
AD/HD, Predominantly Inattentive Type

Six or more of the following symptoms are indicative of ADD without hyperactivity.

1. Difficulty with sustained attention or erratic attention span
2. Easily distracted by extraneous stimuli
3. Excessive daydreaming
4. Disorganized
5. Responds impulsively or without thinking
6. Problems completing things
7. Doesn't seem to listen
8. Shifts from one uncompleted activity to another
9. Often complains of being bored
10. Often appears to be apathetic or unmotivated
11. Frequently sluggish or slow moving
12. Frequently spacey or internally preoccupied

The onset of these symptoms often becomes apparent later in childhood or early adolescence. The brighter the individual, the later symptoms seem to become a problem. The symptoms must be present for at least six months and not be related to a depressive episode or the onset of marijuana usage (Amen, 1997).

Over focused Subtype

Six or more of the following symptoms are indicative of ADD over focused (1 and 2 are needed to make the diagnosis).

1. Difficulty with sustained attention or erratic attention span
2. Easily distracted by extraneous stimuli
3. Excessive or senseless worrying
4. Disorganized or super organized
5. Oppositional, argumentative
6. Strong tendency to get locked into negative thoughts, having the same thought over and over

7. Tendency toward compulsive behavior
8. Intense dislike for change
9. Strong tendency to hold grudges, to hold onto hurts from the past
10. Trouble shifting attention from subject to subject
11. Difficulties seeing options in situations
12. Tendency to hold onto own opinion and not listen to others
13. Tendency to get locked into a course of action, whether or not it is good for the person
14. Becoming very upset if things are not done in a certain way
15. Others complain that you worry too much

Limbic Subtype

Six or more of the following symptoms are indicative of ADD depressive subtype (1 and 2 are needed to make the diagnosis).

1. Difficulty with sustained attention or erratic attention span
2. Easily distracted by extraneous stimuli
3. Moodiness
4. Negativity
5. Low energy
6. Irritability
7. Social isolation
8. Hopelessness, helplessness, excessive guilt
9. Disorganization
10. Lowered sexual interest
11. Sleep changes (too much or too little)
12. Forgetfulness
13. Low self-esteem

Temporal Lobe Subtype

Six or more of the following symptoms are indicative of ADD violent, explosive (1 and 2 are needed to make the diagnosis).

1. Difficulty with sustained attention or erratic attention span
2. Easily distracted by extraneous stimuli
3. Impulse control problems
4. Short fuse or periods of extreme irritability
5. Periods of rages with little provocation
6. Often misinterprets comments as negative when they are not
7. Irritability builds, then explodes, then recedes; often tired after a rage
8. Periods of spaciness or confusion
9. Periods of panic or fear for no specific reason
10. Visual changes, such as seeing shadows or objects changing shape
11. Frequent periods of déjà vu (feelings of being somewhere before even though you never have)
12. Sensitivity or mild paranoia
13. History of a head injury or family history of explosiveness
14. Dark thoughts; may involve suicidal or homicidal thoughts
15. Periods of forgetfulness or memory problems

Another method for assessing older adult ADD is through screening questionnaires.

One of those is The Wender Utah Rating Scale (Wender, 1987). The older adult is asked to describe his or her own experiences. It is recommended that the counselor obtain observations of the client's childhood behaviors from parents, if alive, friends, spouses, and family members. The scale is used to establish continued experiences in:

a. Persistent motor activity

b. Attention deficits and evidence of two or more of the following:
c. Mood swings
d. Inability to complete tasks
e. Inability to control temper
f. Impulsivity
g. Intolerance to stress

Amen's (1997) checklists can be found completely reproduced in the appendix.

There are several other rating scales presented in the appendix and briefly described here. While there is an increasing number of rating scales available there is lack of wide-scale studies to validate them as stand-alone diagnostic instruments. Rating scales are an important part of data collection; however, they do not diagnose a condition (Brunk, 2000).

The University of Massachusetts Medical Center (UMMC) ADD scale is a detailed assessment tool used for adult diagnosis (Barkley, 1990). A partner or close friend is requested to be part of the interview. They are asked to fill out a checklist.

Nadeau (1991) developed a structured interview, which contains 19 categories to measure ADD symptoms in Adults. There are as many as 15 questions in each category. Other assessment tools include Copeland Symptoms Checklist for ADHD (Copeland, 1989) and the Brown Attention-Activation Disorder Scale (Brown and Gammon, 1991).

It is important to note that DSM-IV does not rate levels of ADD as part of the diagnosis. Adults have symptoms with various intensities. These can range from mild, moderate to severe levels. Older adults with mild symptoms can be difficult to identify because older adults often have learned to compensate for their difficulties (Jackson and Farrugia, 1997). It is not clear how much impairment is clinically significant (Roy-Byrne et al. 1997).

Peter Roy-Byrne, et al. (1997) found the Wender Utah Rating Scale (WURS), which answered for both childhood and current ADD symptoms, to be the most discriminating psychometric measure for adult ADD, in comparison to Conner's Continuous Performance Test, The Brief Symptom Inventory/Symptom Checklist and the Social Adjustment Scale.

Rey-Osterrieth Complex Figures (ROCF) were compared to Boston Qualitative Scoring System (BQSS). Adults with ADD showed impairment in measures of configurational accuracy, planning, and neatness. It was concluded that adults with ADD have persistent executive dysfunction; therefore the BQSS may be a useful tool for neuropsychological evaluation of older adults with ADD.

There are some environmental conditions where the symptoms of ADD are absent or minimal for individuals who have the disorder, such as where they are under very strict control and closely directed focus. Examples include when they are engaged in interesting and novel activities or one-on-one situations or under close formal behavioral expectations, such as military activity. It is therefore wise to evaluate the person's behavior in a variety of situations (Khouzam, 1997).

During questioning using a Likert measure process the prototypical symptoms of childhood onset should include questions regarding cognitive difficulties. This includes history of academic under achievement, repeated grades, placement in special classes, and a history of learning disabilities, (Biederman, 1998).

A summary of the symptoms frequently found is (Amen, 1997):

1. Restlessness
2. Problems remaining seated
3. Easily distracted
4. Problems taking turns
5. Responds impulsivity or without thinking
6. Problems completing tasks
7. Difficulty with sustained attention, erratic attention
8. Shifts from one uncompleted activity to another

9. Talks excessively
10. Interrupts frequently
11. Doesn't seem to listen
12. Disorganized
13. Takes high risks
14. Often has poor handwriting
15. Trouble writing
16. Often has difficulty getting to sleep
17. Cannot tune out edges and concentrate on the middle
18. Poor memory
19. Doesn't complete projects
20. Seeks stimulation
21. Easily frustrated
22. Poor eye tracking
23. Poor self-esteem
24. Chronic failure to master social situations
25. Unpleasant reaction from others
26. Suffer from an overdose of criticism
27. Often demoralized and may seem depressed
28. Decreased coordination
29. May have fine motor problems
30. Might have had a bedwetting problem as a child

It is very important when working with older adults that other examinations be conducted to rule out what might appear to be a "normal" aging problem. Other tests should be conducted such as:

- Mental status examination (Folstein, M.F., Folstein, S.E. and McHugh, 1975)
- A mood scale
- Anxiety scale
- Physical examination
- Wechsler memory Scale (WMS-R; Wechsler, 1987)
- Beck depression scale (BDI; Beck, et al. (1961)

Possible co-existing disorders will be discussed in the following chapter.

CHAPTER 4

Differential Diagnosis and Co-morbidity

When an older adult is diagnosed as having ADD, the possibility of other medical problems needs to be evaluated. These medical problems may be misdiagnosed as ADD or they may have ADD and co-existing psychiatric disorders. ADD has an early onset, which requires a review of symptoms and behaviors during childhood in addition to a review of current symptoms. Once it is concluded that an older adult currently has the symptoms of ADD, the assessment should answer two or more questions. First, is this ADD or a medical condition with similar symptoms? Second, is this ADD and a co-existing psychiatric disorder?

Adults having the predominantly inattentive type of ADD can be difficult to diagnose because hyperactivity and impulsivity are the behavior problems most often associated with ADD. Women with ADD tend to have the predominantly inattentive type.

Premenstrual hormonal changes can also interact negatively with ADD and medications used to treat ADD. The typical PMS symptoms of depression and irritability seem to increase for women with ADD. The effects of stimulant medications, which have helped reduce ADD symptoms during other times of the month, lose their effectiveness during this time (Solden, 1995).

The cause of this may be the change in the neurotransmitter, serotonin, which causes PMS symptoms. The change in neurotransmitters that causes PMS may affect the balance between the ADD medication and the neurotransmitters that affect ADD, which is why the stimulant medication does not seem to be working as well for women suffering from PMS. Using another medication to reduce PMS symptoms may allow the stimulant to continue to be effective in the reduction of the ADD symptoms (Ratey, Miller & Nadeau, 1995).

Dr. John Ratey (1992) recommends Prozac and Bu Spar for PMS. He says, "Those medications are used right along with the stimulants, and do not compromise cognitive functioning as other medications have done."

In addition, many of the symptoms of ADD are experienced occasionally by many people and are similar to symptoms of other psychiatric disorders. It is essential that the ADD assessment examine both a differential diagnosis from other similarly symptomatic disorders and the possible existence of co-morbid conditions (Tzelepis, et al. 1995).

Another complicating factor in accurate diagnosis of older adult ADD is the reduction of symptoms. In both long-term follow-up studies of children with ADD and the review of childhood symptoms of adults diagnosed as having had childhood ADD, results indicate that many symptoms ease in adulthood. Symptoms diminish about 50% every 5 years between the ages of 10 and 25 years. Hyperactivity declines more quickly than impulsivity or inattentiveness (Hill, J.C., 1996 and Biederman, J., et al. 1995). However, a longitudinal study of hyperactive children (Barkley, 1996) indicated that approximately 50% function well as adults, whereas the remainder suffer from some degree of impairment in attention, impulse control, problem solving strategies, self-esteem, peer relations, academic attainment, and work record. Barkley (1996) found that 30% to 50% of children with ADD still meet the criteria for ADD as young adults.

There are a number of psychiatric conditions associated with ADD in adults including but not limited to depression, anxiety, and conduct disorder. In considering other conditions that may coexist with ADD in the older adult, it is important to keep in mind that the older a person gets the more likely it is that other conditions may be responsible for the ADD-like conditions (Sudderth and Kandel, 1997).

However, the older adult client should be evaluated for ADD if his or her symptoms are ADD-like. This is especially important for an older adult since it is unlikely he or she are aware that ADD is a lifetime disorder in many individuals. For the same reason most healthcare professionals would not consider ADD as a disorder in this population.

Healthcare professionals may confuse ADD symptoms with PTSD (Post-traumatic Stress Disorder) or illnesses like AIDS (Acquired Immune Deficiency Syndrome), or Lyme disease. Also, ADD may be co-morbid with these disorders and both disorders are related to higher-than-average substance abuse problems (Ouemettee and Najavits, 1998; Wilens, Biedermen, Mick, et al. 1998).

Neurological illnesses may have ADD-like symptoms. This can come from frontal lobe injury through head trauma. Acquired Attention Disorder (ADD-S) resulting from head trauma may respond to the same treatments used for early onset ADD (Mahelick et al. 1998). Also, tumors, strokes, infections, and degenerative diseases (Sudderth and Kandel, 1997) can affect frontal lobes.

Head trauma is a common cause of acquired executive dysfunction, which results in deficiencies in planning, organization, motivation, irritation, mental flexibility, and compulsive control. ADD symptoms in childhood may have been caused by prenatal or postnatal trauma that resulted in ADD. Causes may be gestation, drug use, alcohol or cigarette use, as well as an anoxia at birth, use of forceps during delivery, prematurity, etc., (Lavenstein and Bennett, 1995). Use of forceps at delivery was common prior to 1950 when today's older adults were born.

A physical examination is helpful to distinguish between neurological and psychiatric disorders when older adults appear to be confused. As discussed in Chapter 3 a careful mental status examination should be conducted to assess cognitive impairment. A PET scan might be indicated to rule out drug-induced symptoms vs. a psychiatric disorder.

A neurological screening is very important when diagnosing older adults. For mental health professionals without medical backgrounds, John A. Shinka (1983) developed a Neurological Symptom Questionnaire (NSQ).

Shekim et al. (1990) found that 25% of adults diagnosed with ADD also had Alexithymia which is a neurological disorder marked by loss of the ability to understand written or printed language. Alexithymia is often caused by a brain lesion or congenital defect.

Epilepsy is another disorder, which has some ADD symptoms. Brief forms such as absence seizures and petit mal also exhibit distractibility and inattention (Semund-Clikeman and Wical, 1999). EEG findings and patient history will help distinguish between the presence of ADD or epilepsy.

AIDS, which has spread to the brain, can cause some symptoms similar to ADD. History is again the best way to differentiate between the two conditions.

Tourette's Syndrome is probably the neurological disease with the highest degree of co-morbidity with ADD. The client's history is again the best means to differentiate the two conditions. ADD starts in childhood and continues into adulthood whereas Tourette's Syndrome symptoms frequently fluctuate in severity (Sudderth and Kandel, 1997).

Other diseases that mimic ADD are:

- Lyme disease
- Thyroid disease
- Alzheimer's disease

In a study of adults with ADD, 41% had one or more psychiatric disorders in addition to ADD. Sixty-one percent had a co-morbid condition at some time in their life span and 38% had more than one co-morbid condition (Nadeau, K., 1995). Biederman, et al. (1993) reported that psychiatric comorbidity with ADD could be as high as 77%.

Several studies (Shaywitz, et al. 1995, 1997) found the following co-morbid disorders with ADD:

1. Mood disorders – 10%
2. Conduct disorders – 20%
3. Oppositional defiant disorder – 40%
4. Bipolar disorder – 7%
5. Tourette's syndrome – 60%

Differential diagnosis of older adult ADD may include consideration of agitated depression, hypomania, dissociative disorders, borderline disorder or anti-social personality disorder, alcohol and drug abuse and a variety of primary medical conditions and cognitive brain syndromes (Kane, et al. 1990).

Many conditions can produce ADD-like symptoms including chronic fear, death of a loved one, chronic middle ear infection and abusive situations.

Making a differential diagnosis of mood disorder and ADD is difficult. Ratey et al. (1992) found that mood disorders were the most common diagnosis given adults with ADD who were seen for treatment prior to diagnosis of ADD. Often adults with ADD are misdiagnosed and medicated inappropriately with lithium carbonate, antidepressants and anti-anxiety drugs rather than psychostimulants to reduce ADD symptoms (Ratey et al. 1992).

Many older adults may meet the criteria for both ADD and clinical depression, but may actually be displaying the depressive effects of long term undiagnosed ADD (Resnick, 2000). Clinicians who are not aware of ADD may ascribe the symptoms of inattention, susceptibility to frustration, and susceptibility to depression, to clinical depression. Some distinctions between ADD and depression can be based on symptomatology. Hyperactivity and restlessness caused by ADD may be agitated depression, but a review of the client's history will indicate whether this has been a life-long problem, which is probably due to ADD, or a recent episode, which might be depression. Childhood onset is a key factor in diagnosing ADD. The periodic nature of dysthymia makes it more difficult to differentiate between ADD and dysthymia. The persistence to ADD symptoms when the client does not have the characteristics of dysthymia is a clue that ADD is present. Also, impulsivity and impatience are not typically symptoms of depression. The mood shifts of ADD have neither the enduring quality of major depression nor the magnitude of swings of bi-polar disorder (Nadeau, 1995).

Depression also often includes (Sudderth and Kandel, 1997):

- Lack of motivation
- Changes in social interaction
- Loss of interest in hobbies
- Change in eating or sleeping patterns
- Lack of energy
- Low self-esteem
- Preoccupation with death

With older adults ADD sleep disturbances, anhedonia, and low self-esteem can be enduring qualities present when clinical depression is not. Anhedonia is the lack of the capacity to experience pleasure.

Bi-polar disorder and ADD also have common symptoms. Seven to ten percent of adults with ADD also have bi-polar disorder. The expansive, elevated, or irrational mood of a bi-polar disorder lasts weeks or longer; in ADD these moods last hours to days and have no particular pattern. Grandiosity, which may be delusional, or other psychiatric symptoms are not associated with ADD. Significant reduction in sleep is a manic symptom; ADD affects falling to sleep and awakening early, but not the elimination of sleep. While a person with ADD may be more talkative than usual or interrupting, pressured speech is more likely an indication of bi-polar disorder. Flight of ideas or racing thoughts in bi-polar disorder can be difficult to distinguish from poorly sorted or remembered ideas due to ADD distractibility and inattention. Distractibility, as well as high energy and activity or physical restlessness, can be found in both disorders. Excessive involvement in activities that have high potential for painful consequences can describe people with ADD, especially the impulsive type, but is far more common with bi-polar disorder.

A history of manic episodes and family history of bi-polar disorder will aid in the diagnosis, although bi-polar disorder in a relative of a person with ADD can occur.

Anxiety disorder and ADD also have similar characteristics and often are co-morbid. When an older adult shows inability to cope with common stresses through anxiety symptoms, the cause may be the low frustration tolerance of ADD. Generalized Anxiety Disorder (GAD) mimics ADD more closely than other types. The symptoms, which GAD shares with ADD include restlessness, difficulty concentrating, irritability, muscle tension, and sleep disturbance. Individuals with GAD typically lack the ADD symptoms of impulsivity, disorganization, and attention failure, but may have trouble with concentration and remembering, especially when anxiety is heightened, just as individuals who have ADD do (Sudderth and Kandel, 1997).

Phobias are not generally confused with or associated with ADD symptoms. Likewise, panic disorder and ADD are quite different and virtually never co-morbid. Social phobia however, may be co-morbid in some older adults because of childhood memories involving feelings of embarrassment and humiliation.

Obsessive-Compulsive Disorder (OCD), an anxiety disorder involving ritualistic and often repetitive irrational behavior, is not behavior commonly seen in ADD. Underlying anxieties are present in OCD, but may or may not be present in ADD. Research data are conflicting on how frequently OCD and ADD are co-morbid. It ranges between 4% and 13% (Tzelepis, et al. 1995). What often seems to be compulsive behavior is preoccupation or over-focusing. Adult ADD coping techniques to deal with the disorder may include compulsive behaviors without being driven by an underlying anxiety.

Substance abuse is often a co-morbid disorder with ADD. This is sometimes due to self-medicating to reduce symptoms or relieve the psychological effects from living with ADD symptoms; it may also be due to impulsive and risk taking behavior. It has been reported that 34% of individuals with ADD have histories of alcoholism, 21% for cannabis, 11% for cocaine, and 5% for poly-drug dependence (Shekim, et al. 1990). Individuals with ADD commonly attempt to soothe restless brains with addictive sedating or stimulating substances such as alcohol, marijuana, heroin, prescription tranquilizers and painkillers, or nicotine, caffeine, sugar, cocaine, and street amphetamines. It has been estimated that 30% to 50% of individuals suffering from ADD use drugs and alcohol to self-medicate (Richardson & Wendy, 1999). In addition, people with ADD may develop substance use problems at an earlier age than the general population (Wilens, et al. 1997). It is important to treat both the ADD and the addiction. ADD can interfere with successful recovery from alcohol and drug problems leading to poorer outcome rates after alcohol and drug treatment (Wilens, et al. 1998).

Many adults with ADD exhibit antisocial personality disorders, conduct disorders, and oppositional defiant disorders (Biederman, 1995). Barkley et al. (1990) estimated that 20% to 45% of adults with ADD would also manifest one of these three disorders. This was corroborated in follow-up studies into adulthood of hyperactive children in which antisocial behavior was found later in 18% to 45% (Weiss and Hechtman, 1993).

Disorders such as Conduct Disorder and Oppositional Defiant Disorder significantly increase the risk of substance abuse and Antisocial Personality Disorder in adulthood (Barkley, et al. 1993).

Millon (1981) presented the following traits for sociopathic personality:

1. Hostile affect, illustrated by an irritable temper that flares quickly into argument
2. Social rebelliousness evidenced by contemptuousness toward authority
3. Social vindictiveness displayed by satisfaction when denigrating or humiliating others
4. Fearlessness evident in impulsive behavior and inattention to danger
5. Assertive self-image demonstrated by proudly characterizing oneself as self-reliant and hard-headed
6. Projection of one's own mistrustful and hostile attitudes onto others.

These sociopathic characteristics are similar to childhood Oppositional Defiant Disorder (Tzelepis, et al. 1995). DSM-IV (APA, 1994) defines these behaviors as:

1. Frequent loss of temper
2. Argumentiveness
3. Active defiance of rules or requests of others
4. Intentionally provoking others
5. Blaming others for one's own mistakes
6. Easily annoyed by others
7. Frequent feelings of anger or resentment
8. Being spiteful or vindictive

In addition, anti-social personality disorder or conduct disorder and lesser levels of anti-social behavior may coexist with adult ADD. Tzelepis et al. (1995) found that many adults continued to have oppositional defiant disorder behavior that characterized their childhood and adolescence. Anti-social behavior can be the result of ADD impulsivity, hyperactivity, risk taking, and anti-social learning environment, which may diminish if ADD is treated successfully. In older adults these behaviors may diminish but the underlying attitudes can still be observed.

Schizophrenia has some common symptoms with ADD; however, there are marked differences. Both display poor social relations, lack of motivation, and poor self-esteem, but schizophrenics display delusions, hallucinations, incoherent speech, catatonic behavior and flat affect (APA, 1994). Psychosis is not a feature of ADD.

Borderline Personality Disorder symptoms have a pattern of instability in mood, behavior, relationships, and self-image usually starting in early adulthood (APA, 1994). Symptoms of irritability and impulsivity are shared with ADD symptoms. Prevailing opinion asserts that the two disorders are exclusive of each other (Kane et al. 1990), however, Hooberman and Stern (1984) have suggested there may be co-morbidity of the two disorders.

Some symptoms of Histrionic Personality Disorder overlap those of ADD. These include seeking attention, stimulation, and excitement, impulsivity and over-reaction (Millon,

1981). It is speculated that some of the histrionic characteristics of some individuals are the result of the person's ADD symptoms rather than being a personality disorder (Tzelepis et al. 1995).

Narcolepsy (sleep disorder) and ADD have many similar symptoms. They include poor task execution, poor memory and poor attention. The distinction between ADD and Narcolepsy is based on such ADD symptoms as impulsivity, hyperactivity, inattention and symptoms present in childhood (Sudderth and Kandel, 1997).

Post Traumatic Stress Disorder (PTSD) and ADD have many common symptoms. PTSD occurs after events such as combat, rape, assault, or sexual abuse as children. It has been found that people respond quite differently to exposure to extreme psychological trauma. The severity does not correlate with the degree of reaction (Sudderth and Kandel, 1997). Cause of the disorder has been found to originate from childhood mistreatment, pre-existing psychological disturbance, and alcohol abuse (Sudderth and Kandel, 1997). Persons with PTSD usually avoid experiences that remind them of the episode. This causes them to become hypervigilant, unable to relax, and always on guard. Many of the ADD and PTSD symptoms overlap (Sudderth and Kandel, 1997). Weinstein et al. (2000) discussed PTSD and ADD in sexually abused children. They found a high degree of symptom overlap and co-morbidity between the disorders. They conducted a literature review, which indicated misdiagnosing of ADD in sexually abused children. Since childhood onset is a criterion for ADD and childhood sexual abuse can occur during the same developmental stage, early onset cannot be used to rule out either disorder. History is the best way to differentiate at this time. Childhood traumatic experiences should be investigated to increase accuracy in differential diagnosis.

Another special consideration with older adults is the need to differentiate disease-related psychiatric changes from manifestations of normal aging. Many decrements in capacity or performance, which are viewed as age related are the consequences of an illness and side effects of medication prescribed for the illness (The Merck Manual of Geriatrics, 2000).

ADD can interfere with cognition and be thought to be dementia or senility, but many disorders such as depression and anxiety can also mimic senility. Sleep difficulties are often a result of ADD, but are thought to be part of the normal aging process unless the chronicity and cognitive activities accompanying the sleep difficulty are considered within the ADD framework.

Drug-induced cognitive impairment can mimic many psychiatric disorders including ADD. This is another reason that a complete medical history should be taken and evaluation performed by a health-care professional who is trained in geriatric medicine. Lise (2000) discussed cognitive impairment symptoms in her study, Definition of Drug-Induced Cognitive Impairment in the Elderly. Espino et al. (2000) said, "Poly pharmacy and reactions to medications such as narcotics or benzodiazephines are major causes of confusion in elderly patients." After assessing the four major features of ADD, inattention, distractibility, impulsivity, hyperactivity, and the severity of functional impairment, the counselor must differentiate among possible diagnoses and consider co- morbidity. Only then should a treatment plan be considered.

Chapter 5

Treatment Modalities for Older Adults With ADD

Research has resulted in validating a multi-model approach as the most effective way of treating ADD. The core symptoms of ADD can be reduced with medication. However, social skills, work related problems, and self-esteem generally deteriorate during the life span for those who suffer from ADD, and require a comprehensive treatment plan that addresses all aspects of the person's life (Wender, 1987). Most experts believe that significant, long-lasting benefits come from a combination of medication and behavioral therapy (NIMH, 1996).

Often when adults see an immediate reduction in ADD symptoms, they think medication is all that is needed (NIMH, 1996). There is no cure for ADD known at this time. The goal of treatment is to enhance the individual's ability to cope with the disorder, and intervention should include both medication and psychotherapy as with other chronic mental disorders. The treatment plan should address not only ADD symptoms, but also the client's complete diagnostic profile, including co-morbidity, learning disabilities, neuropsychological dysfunction, and psychosocial difficulties that have arisen from living with ADD (Wender, 1987).

A wide variety of treatments have been used for ADD. They include: psychotropic medication, psychosocial treatment, dietary management, herbal and homeopathic treatments, biofeedback, meditation, and perceptual stimulation training. Of these treatment modalities, stimulant medications and psychosocial interventions have been most accepted and validated by research (NIH, 1998).

A direct, active, informational, structured therapeutic style is recommended with a focus on the places where ADD symptoms affect functioning negatively. The components of treatment should include the following (Amen, 1997):

1. Education
2. Behavior shaping and modifying techniques
3. Goal directed psychotherapy techniques
4. Medication
5. Social skills work
6. Cognitive behavioral therapy
7. Support
8. Sleep management techniques
9. Family effectiveness strategies

Nadeau (1995) has suggested roles for the therapist as an educator, a supporter, an interpreter, a structurer, and a rehabilitation counselor.

Williams and Wilkins (1997) recommend the following treatment plan:

A. Planning

1. Establish target symptoms of ADD and baseline levels of impairment.
2. Consider treatment for co-morbid conditions (monitor possible drug seeking behavior).
3. Prioritize modalities to fit target symptoms and available resources.
4. Monitor multiple domains of functioning.
    a. Academic or vocational.
    b. Daily living skills.
    c. Emotional adjustment.
    d. Family interactions.
    e. Social relationships.
    f. Medication response.
5. Periodically reevaluate the efficacy of and need for additional interventions.
6. Maintain long-term supportive contact with the patient and family to ensure compliance with treatment and to address new problems that arise.

B. Treatment

1. Education for patient, spouse, or other significant persons.
2. Consideration of vocational evaluation, counseling, or training.
3. Medication.
   a. Stimulants.
   b. Tricyclic antidepressants.
   c. Other antidepressants.
   d. Other drugs (buspirone, propranolol).
4. Psychosocial and behavioral interventions.
   a. Individual cognitive therapy; "coaching."
   b. Family psychotherapy if family dysfunction is present.
   c. Referral to support group, such as CHADD (Children and Adults with Attention Deficit/Hyperactivity Disorder).

Education

Education of the client and significant others about ADD is the beginning phase and a very important part of the treatment process. Typically older adults have no knowledge of the disorder. Receiving the diagnosis of ADD can be very helpful to the client since there is an explanation for his or her behavior. Being aware that ADD is a neurological condition and not a behavioral defect is very therapeutic. When the counselor educates the client and significant others about the disorder they experience a feeling of hope and empowerment.

Education of the older adult with ADD consists of learning current information about the disorder. The therapist should keep current on new research including treatment modalities, which can be used to educate their clients. The clinician should describe the signs and symptoms of the disorder and how the intensity of these symptoms varies among individuals. The current thinking about the neuropsychological aspects of the disorder would be helpful information for the client.

The client should be told about the core symptoms of inattention, distractibility and impulsiveness, with or without hyperactivity. They should also learn that the disorder is not a behavioral problem but is a chronic neurological disorder, which often runs in families. It is recommended that the older adult be given a list of suggested books to learn more about ADD. A list can be found in the appendix of this book.

It is helpful for the person suffering from ADD to know what it is and what it is not. Also it is helpful to recognize strengths that are associated with ADD such as: creativity, sense of humor, lack of inhibition, high energy level, often ability to hyper-focus, and willingness to take risks. Problems often related to ADD are: low self-esteem, depression, moodiness, substance abuse, disorganization, anxiety, and difficulties in relationships (Roberts and Jamsen, 1997).

Medication

The next phase of treatment is pharmacotherapy. Medication is usually essential to effective treatment of adult ADD. Without medication other interventions are usually not beneficial. The goals of medication are (Amen, 1997):

- Increase attention span
- Decrease distractibility
- Decrease restlessness or high activity levels
- Decrease impulsiveness and increase thoughtfulness
- Decrease irritability
- Increase motivation
- Improve functioning at home, in relationships and emotional factors within the client

Psychopharmacological trials show that when most adults are treated with stimulants their symptoms are reduced. Over one hundred-fifty randomized controlled studies with more than 5000 participants demonstrated that stimulant medication effectively alleviated ADD symptoms for 65 to 75% of those diagnosed with ADD (Spencer et al. 1996; Greenhill, et al. 1999). While most of the studies were done on children, the same medication works well on adults.

Neurobiological findings in adult ADD have been described, including brain Positron Emission Topography (PET) scans that revealed reduced glucose metabolism in areas of the cerebral cortex associated with control of attention and motor activity (Zamethkin et al. 1990). These findings support the theory that ADD is a central nervous system disorder.

Since ADD is believed to be a central nervous system disorder, medications that affect the central nervous system seem to be the most effective in reducing symptoms. Stimulant medications are the primary pharmacological treatment for adults who are diagnosed as having ADD. Studies have shown that stimulants block the reuptake of dopamine and norepinephrine into the presynaptic neuron (Nadeau, 1995). In a 7-week study of 23 adults with ADD, a 78% positive response was noted for methylphenidate hydrochloride (Ritalin) (Nadeau, 1995).

The following list shows the stimulants generally used for treating ADD (Amen, 1997):

1. Methylphenidate (Ritalin)
2. Methylphenidate sustained release (Ritalin SR)
3. Amphetamine salt combination (Adderall)
4. Dextroamphetamine (Dexedrine)
5. Dextroamphetamine slow-release caps (Dexedrine Spansules)
6. Methamphetamine (Desoxyn)
7. Pemoline (Cylert)

Other types of medication may be used if stimulants do not work or if ADD occurs with another disorder. Antidepressants may be used to alleviate depression co-existing with ADD. These are not first line medications for ADD, however they are often used in conjunction with a stimulant for co-existing disorders such as depression or anxiety. The following is a list of tricyclic antidepressants and bupropion, which can be used if stimulants do not reduce the symptoms of ADD. These are usually the second line medications for ADD (Amen, 1997):

1. Disipramine (Norpramin)

2. Imipramine (Tofranil)
3. Bupropion (Wellbutrin)
4. Bupropion sustained release (Wellbutrin SR)
5. Amitryslyline (Clavil)
6. Nortriptyline (Pamelor)
7. Doxepin (Sinequan)
8. Clomipramine (Anafranil)

Anti-obsessive medication can be used as a third line of medication as listed below (Amen, 1997).

(Note: these also are not first line medications and sometimes make ADD symptoms worse.)

1. Fluoxetine (Prozac)
2. Clomipramine (Anafranil)
3. Sertraline (Zoloft)
4. Paroxetine (Paxil)
5. Fluvoxamine (Luvox)
6. Venlafaxine (Effexor)
7. Mirtazapine (Remeron)

Anticonvulsants or anti-seizure medications sometimes used in conjunction with stimulants are listed below (Amen, 1997). (Note: They are often helpful if brain trauma occurred.)

1. Carbamazepine (Tegretol)
2. Valproic acid (Depakene)
3. Divalproex (Depakote)
4. Gabapentin (Neurontin)
5. Lamotrigine (Lamictal)
6. Phenytoin (Dilantin)

Blood pressure medications that affect anxiety are listed below (Amen, 1997).

1. Clonidine (Catapres)
2. Guanfacine (Tenex)
3. Propranolol (Inderal)

Often combinations of medications are needed to obtain full symptom reduction. A combination of stimulants and other medications is sometimes the most effective way to treat some clients.

Barkley (1990) has reported that approximately 30% to 50% of adult ADD clients do not respond well to psychostimulants alone, sometimes because of side effects or because co-morbid depressive and anxiety disorders are exacerbated.

Determining the dosage for older adults when using psychotropic medications should be done considering the following differences between younger adults and older adults (Merck Manual, 2000).

1. The same dose of psychoactive drug usually takes longer to work
2. The drug remains in the body longer
3. The drug may produce a greater effect on an older person than a younger person.

The five areas of pharmacokinetics (how the body handles the drug) need to be considered when prescribing medication for older adults (Merck Manual, 2000): absorption, distribution, metabolism, excretion and CNS sensitivity.

Absorption: Most psychoactive drugs are absorbed through the intestinal mucosa. Aging usually does not alter absorption; however, other prescribed or over-the-counter drugs can interfere with how well the drugs are absorbed and how fast.

Distribution: Often body fat increases with age and total body water decreases. This may cause increased storage of the drug requiring lower doses and changes in frequency of administration.

Metabolism The liver metabolizes many psychoactive drugs. With aging, often the liver metabolizes at a slower rate causing the drug to remain in the system longer, hence requiring smaller doses.

Excretion Renal function is often reduced with aging, causing the drug to remain in the system longer.

CNS sensitivity Increased CNS receptors may require reduced dosage for older adults.

Psychotherapy

Some professionals question the place of psychotherapy in geriatric medicine, but its efficacy has been demonstrated in numerous older patients (Merck Manual of Geriatrics, 1994).

Since people are living longer it is even more important to provide psychotherapy for the older adults. A 65-year-old may live 20 or more additional years.

Without proper medication, psychotherapy treatment is unlikely to be of benefit. It may be a fruitless and frustrating experience for both the therapist and the client, who already has feelings of frustration and hopelessness (Amen, 1997). Psychotherapy as well as education may be necessary to eliminate the feeling that taking medication is bad.

When medication intervention stabilizes the ADD symptoms, psychotherapy is needed to resolve emotional and behavioral problems resulting from having ADD and to teach strategies to change patterns developed over a lifetime.

Many older adults have developed coping skills, which enable them to function. The next chapter will address these coping skills.

Many older adults with ADD have experienced a multitude of ADD-related discouraging and frustrating events during their lifetime. They have often felt an inner sense of underachievement and frustration. They have received negative messages from family members, teachers, spouses, employers, and children about their weaknesses and shortcomings, which has resulted in low self-esteem.

There is a common feeling of "learned helplessness", a sense that no matter what they do it will not be right (Seligman, 1990). A high percentage of adult clients with ADD admit to low self-esteem; they often feel they have a character defect, which deflates their self-confidence (Nadeau, 1995). The symptoms of inattentiveness, impulsivity, interrupting others, temper, and mood swings cause relationship problems and make it difficult to keep friends.

Part of the treatment should include cognitive reframing the past so that they can see the past differently having learned the symptoms of their disorder. Inaccurate ideas resulting from past experiences should be reframed into a more positive light in order to help the client rebuild his or her self-esteem and feel that the situation can be improved by proper treatment modalities (Nadeau, 1995). Seligman's

(1991, 1995) learned optimism model based on changing one's cognitive explanatory style regarding the permanence, pervasiveness, and personal responsibility for them can be useful, given the all-or-nothing thinking of many adults with ADD

Without psychotherapy the client is likely to continue to commit the same errors and observe the same self-defeating and inappropriate patterns of behavior. The goals of psychotherapy should be to alleviate emotional distress, to train the client to recognize unhealthy patterns that have developed over a lifetime, and to help him or her change those patterns. Often a person with ADD will be unable to recognize his or her social ineptness, which those with whom they associate see very clearly. Family therapy may be needed when relationships have become reactive and cooperation is low. The therapist can help the client change erroneous belief patterns, including the belief that they have always failed in school and work, are meant to have poor relationships, and always will.

Amen (1997) gave examples of negative thoughts:

- I'm a terrible student or employee
- I'm always messing things up
- No one ever wants to be with me
- Anybody could have done that. I'm not so special
- The teacher (or boss) doesn't like me
- I will fail at this
- I feel you don't love me
- I should do better
- I'm so stupid

Cognitive-behavioral therapy seems most appropriate for older adults with ADD. Clients can work on immediate issues. It helps clients to help themselves by changing their behavior. The interventions should include (Jackson and Farrugia, 1997):

(a) educating the client
(b) developing attention management skills

(c) developing self-management skills
(d) developing interpersonal skills
(e) developing anger management skills
(f) developing problem solving skills
(g) developing stress management skills

Many older adults have developed coping skills, which enable them to function by attenuating their ADD symptoms. Recognition of this accomplishment can be used to encourage them to use therapy to reduce other frustrations. Self-generated coping skills will be addressed further in the next chapter.

Group counseling is best for this social skills training. Group counseling can offer a great opportunity for the older adult to learn more about social and interpersonal skills and for social skills training (Hallowell, 1994). It also allows them to realize that others have the same issues.

Individual therapy can help older adults modify their behavior using social skills training. The therapist can discuss and model appropriate behaviors, such as not interrupting others, or not letting anger escalate, and then practice these skills with the client (NIMH, 1996).

Researchers have found that adults with ADD may have problems creating and sustaining healthy social and interpersonal relationships (Herrero, et al. 1994). Problems with inattention, impulsivity, and all-or-nothing thinking, along with disorganized thought patterns, impair social performance (Guevremont, 1990). ADD adults who monitor their own behavior become more productive (Nadeau, 1995). Self-control training will aid in social skill performance. Self-awareness is the first step toward self-management (Jackson and Farrugia, 1997); clients are trained to self-monitor. The therapist can help the older adult client become aware of dysfunctional lifelong habits. Then they can concentrate on target behaviors, one step at a time, to reach mutually established goals (Nadeau, 1995). Becoming aware of their personal strengths and weaknesses and using constructive self-talk can help self-control. This is a good time to introduce the client to coaching and to encourage him or her to select a coach. Coaching will be discussed more completely in the next two chapters.

The client can learn to control attention by techniques such as focused attention, sustained attention, selective attention, alternating attention, and divided attention (Jackson & Farrugia, 1997). Techniques for time management are timing attention span, learning how long they can pay attention, and use of this information to improve concentration (DuPaul and Stoner, 1994). They can break tasks into small units to match their attention span.

The counselor can assist the older adult client by training in performance management. Nadeau (1995) recommends advising them to make use of:

- Lists
- Notes to self
- Color coding
- Rituals
- Reminders
- Files

A very important issue for the older adult client with ADD is to practice mood management. They can be helped to become aware of their mood changes and learn to control them. One significant area is anger management; many older adults with ADD have low frustration tolerance and this frustration may build into explosive behaviors (Leimkuhler, 1995). DuPaul and Stoner (1994) suggest a model for anger control training. Clients are trained to recognize environmental events that lead to frustration and anger and internal events that are associated with anger (Jackson and Farrugia, 1997).

DuPaul and Stoner (1994) outlined the following steps for anger reduction training.

1. Recognize internal cues associated with anger
2. Use coping self-statements to inhibit open expression of anger
3. Generate a plan for responding to provocation

4. Have a self-reinforced contingency plan if one becomes too angry to deal with a situation.

Other significant mood problems for older adults with ADD are depression and pessimism. Years of frustration can condition a negative internalized response. Seligman's (1991, 1995) learned optimism model presents one useful approach, using cognitive therapy theory to alter experiences from permanent to temporary, pervasive to specific, and from personal to external.

Stress management training should be a part of the client's training. An older adult with ADD suffers from many stressful events living with the symptoms. The counselor can help the clients identify the sources of stress in their lives and learn to recognize them. Positive self-talk is one helpful method (Hallowell, 1995). Stress inoculation methods are also useful (Beck, 1995).

Problem-solving skill training can be very helpful for the older adult client. Nadeau (1995) outlined the following steps for counselor assistance:

- Define the problem in a careful verbal analysis, which may lead to a new or modified definition of the problem
- Propose alternative solutions through a process of brainstorming
- Select the best solution among the proposed alternative solutions
- Attempt the selected solution
- Analyze the results of the attempt
- Propose an alternative solution if the initial results were not satisfactory
- Analyze the results of the second solution

In concluding this chapter it seems appropriate to again repeat the concern that older adult ADD is rarely considered in therapy settings and as a result the condition goes untreated while the severity of symptoms increases (Jackson and Farrugia, 1997).

When an older adult suffering from ADD seeks help it is often other issues, such as being fired, relationship problems, memory problems, etc., which precipitate his or her decision. The initial contact may have been to address these problems. The counselor is encouraged to keep in mind the possibility of ADD as an underlying factor in other psychiatric difficulties (Jackson and Farrugia, 1997).

In addition to psychotherapy there are many self-help techniques that can be extremely helpful for the older adult who suffers from ADD. This is the topic of the next chapter.

CHAPTER 6

Self-help Techniques for Older Adults with ADD

This chapter provides mental health professionals with information and methods to help older adults who have been diagnosed with ADD to learn self-help skills. Retraining dysfunctional behavior patterns is an essential part of the treatment for ADD (Amen, 1997) as ADD causes many learned behaviors and cognitive thought patterns that are faulty and harmful.

Often people with ADD have been given negative feedback about their behavior for years from parents, teachers, friends, spouses, children and others. A lifetime of negative feedback can cause individuals to develop internal criticism, which is often automatically switched on when receiving criticism from others. This in turn causes defensive behavior, which may escalate into anger and lower self-esteem. Individuals with ADD make mistakes because of inattention, impulsivity, forgetting, and faulty habits which lead to internal criticism and criticism from others.

To stimulate their brains many older adults having ADD have learned to upset others. They are unaware on a conscious level of the connection between the relief they receive from the increase in their brain activity and their confrontation with others and they are likely to deny that they do it.

ADD negatively affects many life issues of older adults, including physical, emotional, financial, and social issues. Older adults who have ADD commonly do not take care of their general health due to inattention and forgetting. Hyperfocusing,concentrating on one issue to the exclusion of others, also causes ADD sufferers to neglect taking medication at the proper time and to be inconsistent with other health matters such as eating, hygiene and sleep.

Prochaska, Norcross, and DiClemsute (1994) found after extensive research that the change process is composed of six stages. They are:

1. Pre-contemplation (change is avoided and problems are denied)
2. Contemplation (the need for change is accepted and information is sought)
3. Preparation (plans are made)
4. Action (plans are implemented)
5. Maintenance (success is solidified)
6. Termination (new behaviors are internalized and accepted; therefore efforts to change can be stopped)

Habit substitution is a method for behavioral modification. The clinician helps the client identify undesired habits he or she wishes to change and positive behavioral habits, which can be substituted for them (Sudderth and Kandel, 1997).

Steps for changing/shaping behavior are listed below (Amen, 1997):

1. Define the desired and undesirable behaviors
2. Clearly communicate the things that rile them and their expectations
3. Establish a baseline period
4. Reward desired behavior

In addition to negative response patterns, older adults usually have developed many coping skills in order to live with their disorder. Habit substitution can be built upon these coping skills, recognizing them as strengths and indications that the person can succeed further in behavior changes. To elicit a client's coping behavior, questions can be helpful such as (Wells, Dahl, Snyder, 2000):

What helps you get through repetitive tasks?

*Using deadlines for structure
* Using last-minute pressure to get energized
* Delegating to another person
* Doing a small amount of the task at a time
* Working with another person
* Varying tasks – doing several things at the same time
* Setting up rituals
* Persisting

What helps you control your impulses?

* Talking to yourself
* Switching gears mentally, thinking of something else
* Switching gears physically, leaving the situation

What helps you avoid environmental distractions?

* Going to a quiet place, isolating yourself
* Using background "white" noise such as music or television
* Hyper-focusing

What helps you control the intensity of unpleasant feelings?

* Taking time out mentally to talk to yourself or with another person
* Taking time out physically, going for a walk or exercise
* Leaving the situation

What helps you when you try to fix a problem and fail?

* Getting away, putting it out of your mind and re-focusing on the problem later
* Talking to others or to yourself
* Delegating the task to someone else

What helps you retain large amounts of information?

* Taking notes
* Using flash cards for schoolwork
* Watching someone else and then doing it, not relying on written instructions
* Asking questions and linking the idea or task to something that is already known
* Going to a quiet place and hyper-focusing
* Working on chunks of material at a time

What helps you stay organized?

* Making notes to yourself (lists, post-its, calendar, daily planner)
* Goal setting – structure each day (use mental mapping)

* Prioritizing
* Doing lots of projects at any one time
* Piling things and paper
* Delegating
* Pressure to get it done

What do you need in a job to help you feel satisfied in it?

* Action every day – every day has a new routine
* Many tasks at one time
* Dealing with different people all the time
* Sense of accomplishment – pats on the head
* Being creative
* Being in charge of myself and my time
* Quick fixes – work that can be accomplished with quick burst of energy
* Structure
* Quotas and pressure

What helps you maintain relationships with family and friends?

* Maintaining eye contact when talking
* Asking questions so they know you are listening and interested
* Talking out your feelings with someone else
* Stepping back mentally and physically, going to another room

Improving attention and concentration is a very important aspect of helping an individual with ADD. Sohlberg and Mateer (1989) developed a model with five levels of attention:

1. Focused attention: the ability to respond discretely to specific stimuli
2. Sustained attention: the ability to maintain a consistent behavioral response during continuous repetitive activity
3. Selective attention: freedom from distractibility
4. Alternating attention: mental flexibility, the ability to shift focus ofattention between tasks having different cognitive requirements

5. Divided attention: ability to respond simultaneously to multiple tasks or multiple task demands

When working with attention issues of older adults with ADD, the clinician will be aware of distractibility and problems with focus and sustained attention, but may need to question the client to uncover the more complex and often unavoidable problems with alternating and divided attention. Often the highly intelligent, higher functioning adults with ADD have learned to focus and sustain their attention, which has allowed them to be academically successful. These same adults, however, can still have significant difficulty with the complex demands for divided and alternating attention placed upon them as they are promoted to positions as supervisor, project manager, or department head (Nadeau, 1995).

Parente and Andersen-Parente (1991) listed several attention-enhancing strategies, which are helpful with the first three levels of attention:

1. Frequent self-monitoring: "What should I be doing now?"
2. Assigning time: setting scheduled time to ponder thoughts that repetitively intrude into thoughts regarding the current task
3. Allowing activity: engaging in physical movement while listening or memorizing
4. Distributing practice sessions: taking frequent breaks
5. Active learning: repeating material heard or read, restating in own words
6. Building incentives for concentration: scheduling small rewards earned by periods of concentrated study

Parente and Andersen-Parente (1991) also list several methods that are helpful in focusing.

1. Making lists
2. Setting deadlines
3. Making schedules
4. Breaking tasks into smaller steps

5. Pacing one's self
6. Making planned transition

Memory retention is one of the most important but less attended cognitive deficiency experienced by individuals with ADD. The inability to retain one's thoughts plays an important role in why many people with ADD interrupt: they are afraid they will not remember their thoughts if they don't blurt them out when they think of them. Focused and sustained attention is critical to memory. The older adult with ADD with high distractibility may never make the initial step of paying attention to incoming information and therefore may never acquire it (Nadeau, 1995). Memory is extremely important when working with older adults, where poor memory caused by ADD may be misdiagnosed as dementia.

Memory problems in the ADD older adult can cause significant difficulties with co-workers, friends, spouses, and family members.

Memory training and coping techniques include (Nadeau, 1995):

1. Daily calendar (day timers)
2. Electronic reminders
3. Visual prompts
4. Routines
5. Having a piece of paper and pencil available to take notes when the thought presents itself. This can help to reduce interrupting others; the other person needs to be informed that the person with ADD is doing this to avoid interrupting rather than being thought of as not paying attention to them.
6. Checkbook. Use of a checkbook slows down the purchase process so that the person with ADD has time to think about the purchase.
7. Beepers can be used to locate and remind the individual of appointments.
8. Hand held recorders could help by allowing the person to store their thoughts when they occur.

9. Palm recorders can be used to record appointments, special dates, etc.
10. Fax machines, answering machines and cellular phones all are very useful for the person with ADD.
11. Many other high tech devices such as computers, financial software, etc., can be very helpful for adults with ADD. For many older adults these are not items they want to learn to use. Low self-esteem and previous failures may interfere.

Time management training can be very useful for the older adult with ADD. If the person is still working, time management will help with work related tasks. If the person is retired, time management might be even more difficult because of the loss of daily routines, such as going to work at the same time every day and being required to pay attention to what day it is. Using day timers is very helpful. Some competence with focused and sustained attention is needed to effectively use day timers (Nadeau, 1995):

1. The first step is to keep the day timer up to date.
2. Learn to note all schedules and commitments in the day timer.
3. "Do-it-now." Note it in the day timer when the schedule is committed.
4. Write the schedules in the day timer only, not elsewhere.
5. Be specific in regard to the date, time, and task.
6. Do not schedule too many tasks.
7. Give sufficient time to complete the task. Consider the time it takes to move from one task to another. This may include travel time, accumulating data, interruptions, and underestimating the time required to complete the task.

Methods for shifting focus from one activity to another, alternating attention will help persons with ADD who often has difficulty transitioning between activities. Setting times for the telephone to beep is a method that works well for some people. Having someone else, such as a secretary or a coach, remind the person with ADD that they need to stop what they are doing and move to another task, is very helpful if available.

Many adults with ADD are chronically late as a result of difficulty in shifting or sustaining focus. The attention problems that interfere with timeliness include (Nadeau, 1995):

1. Over commitment
2. Distractibility
3. Hyper-focusing
4. Living reactively rather than proactively

Avoidance, denial and procrastination are some negative behavior patterns developed by adults with ADD. These can be caused by (Nadeau, 1995):

1. Being unable to say no when asked to do something
2. Being too reactive, in an unplanned mode.
3. Being poor at performing tasks requiring organizational skills, such as writing reports, doing income tax preparation, balancing the checkbook, filing material, getting rid of piles of papers, etc.

Organizing their environment can help the person with ADD to cope with attention and memory tasks, and to develop self-efficacy. For example:

1. Putting items in the same place all the time
2. Filing papers and throwing away unneeded papers on a regular basis

Amen (1997) suggested the following methods to help the person with ADD with organizational problems and procrastination:

Practical/Organizational:

** Make clear goals for your life in the following areas:

- relationships (spouse/lover, children, family and friends)
- work
- money
- physical health
- emotional health
- spirituality

Ask oneself, "Is my behavior getting me what I want?" What is needed to accomplish personal goals?

** Manage your time in a way that is consistent with the goals you have for your life.

** Take the extra time to organize your work area on a regularly scheduled basis. Devote some time each week to organization. Otherwise procrastination will take over.

** Use the FRAT system in organizing paper flow: (keep up with the paper work or have someone do it for you)

File it
Route it
Action
Throw it away

** Prioritize your projects.

** Make deadlines for yourself.

** Keep TO DO lists and revise them on a regular basis.

** Keep an appointment and planning book with you.

** Use a portable cassette recorder to remember ideas throughout the day.

** Break down large tasks into a series of smaller ones. Do a little each day on a certain project.

** Use file folders, desk organizers and labeled storage boxes to organize your paperwork.

Amen (1995) offers this advice to reduce procrastination:

1. Consciously fight procrastination. The sooner you do it, the sooner it will be done. If you can do it now, then do it now.
2. Break down overwhelming tasks into small tasks. This happens on assembly lines every day. Remember, "A journey of a thousand miles begins with one step."
3. Do a start-up task now! Go to the next step you need to do to accomplish that goal and do it. Just getting started will increase your momentum.
4. Make a wager with someone. Use your competitive nature to your advantage.
5. Give yourself a reward. Tell yourself that after you finish a difficult task, you'll reward yourself with something special you want.

6. Do unpleasant tasks first. That way, you'll have the more pleasurable ones to look forward to. If you save the unpleasant tasks for last, you'll have little incentive to get to them.
7. Tell someone else the date that you'll finish. Putting your word or reputation on the line is often an incentive to get started.
8. Think about how you will feel once the task is done. Anticipating the sense of accomplishment will help spur you on.

Stress has a strong negative influence on an older adult with ADD. Periods of increased demands, fatigue, illness, conflict, and frustration are often times in which the manifestations of attention deficit disorder are exacerbated (Nadeau, 1997). Stress results in less organization, more forgetfulness, more mistakes, and more anger. Many individuals with ADHD (hyperactive) are attracted to highly stimulating environments, despite their low tolerance to stress. The clinician needs to help the client identify his or her stressors and to find ways to reduce stress. The older adult often has many stressors due to the aging process, such as retiring, possible indebtedness, reduction in income, medical problems, and changes in the environment. The clinician can help the client identify stressors, many of which are exacerbated by ADD related behaviors. These might include (Nadeau, 1997):

1. Finances
   - Indebtedness
   - Impulse purchases
   - Poor record keeping
   - Lack of planning and budgeting
   - Retirement
2. Family
   - Marital problems
   - Child behavior problems
   - Inconsistent parenting
   - Family crises: illnesses, death, divorce
3. Career
   - Workplace stress

Interpersonal conflicts on the job
Poor job match
Traffic/long commute
Long work hours

4. Health-related stressors
   Poor health
   Poor diet/exercise habits
   Sleep disturbance
5. General stressors
   Domino effect: unsolved problems creating new problems
   Chronic over-commitment
   Poor time management
   Poor organization
   Too many major life changes
6. Internal stressors
   Fear of failure
   Feelings of inadequacy
   Distractibility
   Disorganization

Stress reduction includes helping the client develop more constructive life management skills (Nadeau, 1997):

1. Stress reduction through simplifying by:
   a. Looking for ways to live on one and one-half-incomes rather than two, allowing more time at home for the performance of household and family duties
   b. Changing jobs to gain a shorter commute
   c. Avoiding rush hour commuting through flextime
   d. Agreeing to set aside some portion of the dual income to pay for services such as house cleaning, home repairs, and lawn mowing, thereby reducing the demand level at home
2. Stress reduction through delegating tasks. If the client has a significant other, tasks may be divided equally according to ability and preference.

Also, some tasks may best be accomplished by hiring someone.

3. Stress reduction through stimulation management. Noise and large crowds can be very stressful for adults with ADD. Adjusting shopping times to off-hours, or finding a quiet place to relax after exposure to high activity and noise may help the client to relax before interacting with others.
4. Stress reduction through learning tolerance. It is helpful to learn techniques to better tolerate stress. These include regular exercise, relaxation techniques, and meditation.

Many older adults have problems with waking and sleeping cycles. Aging problems and/or ADD can cause this. Since this is so common with adults who have ADD, the clinician should determine if this has been a problem throughout the client's life cycle or started in older adulthood.

For adults with ADD-related sleep problems, getting up in the morning can be the worst. Many people with ADD feel very groggy or fuzzy headed in the morning (Amen, 1997). Adults frequently use coffee as a stimulant "to get them started in the morning."

Amen (1997) listed some helpful ways to assist adults with ADD-related sleep problems:

1. Go to bed at a reasonable time
2. Find an alarm clock that plays the kind of music that gets the person going. Try different forms of music to see what works best.
3. Keep the alarm clock (or clocks) across the room so that the person has to get out of bed to turn it off.
4. Take ADD medicine a half-hour before getting out of bed.
5. Have something to do that motivates him or her in the morning. Some people enjoy working out with weights in the morning as a way to get their bodies (and brains) feeling alive.

6. Stay away from early morning activities if possible.
7. Watch the body's own cycle. Some people are good in the morning and some later on. Fit your schedule to your body's rhythms.

Going To Bed

Some people with ADD "go and go" all day until they drop from exhaustion. Others have difficulty getting to sleep; still others wake up frequently throughout the night, or they are hyperactive in their sleep and constantly on the move. The ADD person, who is often very hard to wake up, becomes even more difficult to wake up in the morning and is certainly more irritable with a poor night's sleep.

Researchers aren't sure why people with ADD have more sleep problems. Some think it has to do with a brain chemical called serotonin. When there is not enough of this "sleep chemical," there is more of a problem.

Amen (1995) gives these suggestions for getting to sleep:

1. Eliminate television 1 – 2 hours before bedtime, especially any program that may be over stimulating (the shows you most like). This includes news programs, since people with ADD tend to ruminate on the bad things that happened that day in their own world and the world at large.
2. Stimulating, active play should be eliminated for 1 – 2 hours before bedtime, such as wrestling, tickling, teasing, etc. Quiet activities are more helpful in the hours before bedtime, such as reading, drawing, or writing.
3. Some people try to read themselves to sleep. This can be helpful. But read boring books. If you read action-packed thrillers or horror stories you are not likely to drift off into peaceful never-never land.
4. A warm, quiet bath is often helpful.

5. A bedtime back rub in bed may be soothing. Starting from the neck and working down in slow rhythmic strokes can be very relaxing.
6. Soft, slow music often helps people drift off to sleep. Instrumental music, as opposed to vocal, seems to be the most helpful. Some people with ADD say that they need fast music in order to block out their thoughts.
7. Nature sound tapes (rain, thunder, ocean, rivers) can be very helpful as well as "white noise" like the sound of fans.
8. For some people with ADD restrictive bedding is helpful, such as a sleeping bag or being wrapped tightly in blankets.
9. A mixture of warm milk, a tablespoon of vanilla (not imitation vanilla, the real stuff), and a table-spoon of sugar can be very helpful. This increases serotonin to the brain and helps promote sleep.
10. Self-hypnosis can be a powerful tool for aiding sleep. Here's a quick self-hypnosis course:
    a. Focus your eyes on a spot and count slowly to 20… let your eyes feel heavy as you count and close them as you get to 20.
    b. Take three or four very slow, deep breaths.

Tighten the muscles in your arms and legs and then let them relax. Imagine yourself walking down a staircase while you count backwards from 10 (this will give you the feeling of "going down" or becoming sleepy. With all of your senses (sight, touch, hearing, taste, smell), imagine a very sleepy scene, such as lying by a fire in a mountain cabin or in a sleeping bag at the beach.

The different medications used to promote sleep include:

1. Over-the-counter medications such as Benadryl, Unisom, Sominex, Excedrin PM, Nyquil, etc.
2. Some antidepressants, such as imipramine (Tofranil), amitriptyline (Elavil), or trazone (Desyrel)

(trazodone is used only in females; in men it may cause painful erections that will not go away.) Often these are used in very low doses to help promote sleep. They are helpful to people who have a tendency toward depression.

3. Certain blood pressure medications such as clonidine (Catapres). Clonidine is sometimes used to calm down the restlessness or hyperactivity that often goes along with ADD.
4. Sleeping medications, such as temazepam (Restoril), triazolam (Halcion), zolpidem (Ambien), flurazepam (Dalamane), estazolam (ProSom). These medications tend to lose their effectiveness after a few weeks. They should be used on a short-term basis only.

There are many self-help resources, some of which are listed in the appendix. Some of these are Nadeau's Top 10 Traps in the Workplace; Amen's Effective Behavior Shaping and Modifying Techniques; Roberts and Jamsen's Living with ADD: A work book for Adults with ADD, and organizations such as; CHADD, ADDA, etc.

The last technique to be presented in this chapter is coaching. This is a very important element for the ADD older adult person and a good way to help with social skills training. Adults with ADD are known to have poor self-observation skills. It is important to find someone who can give constructive feedback and encourage the person with ADD to learn new habits (Roberts and Jamsen, 1997).

Sudderth and Kandel (1997) said, "Life coaches," are the ultimate adaptive device. A coach can be a paid assistant or a life partner or spouse. Utilizing the significant other's strengths in organization, day planning, and interpretation can be very helpful. Not only does he or she know the most about the client, but also it will help the non-ADD person to learn more about the disorder and buy into the improvement motivation of the person with ADD. If a partner is not the best choice for the specific client, a friend can be an excellent choice to coach the client.

It is important for ADD individuals and their partners to add some behavior changes to stabilize the relationship (Solden, 1995). The non-ADD partner can become an active partner in helping the ADD person to change old habits and strengthen the relationship by working together to improve their relationship.

The main areas where a coach can help are to keep the ADD person on track, help identify when the ADD person is not on track, and by being supportive. He or she can help the person with ADD recognize his or her successes. Also, the coach can help maintain systems designed to aid in habit changes.

Hallowell and Ratey (1994) stated that they "particularly liked the idea of a coach." The person may also be a therapist, but does not need to be. They (Hallowell and Ratey) suggest organizing the coach objectives as follows:

H - Help – Ask what kind of help is needed

O - Obligations – Ask what obligations are coming up

P - Plans – Ask about ongoing plans

E - Encouragement – This is the most important function of the coach.

Several organizations provide training for coaches. CHADD and ADDA are two of the most popular. Others can be found in the appendix. Andrea Little (2000) Board of Directors member of ADDA, defines the job of coaching thus: "ADD coaching is an on-going relationship, which focuses on the client taking action toward the realization of their vision, goals or desires. ADD coaching uses a process of inquiry to discover ways in which a client can maximize strengths and talents, function optimally with a disability, and be responsible and accountable for actions, or lack of action. ADD coaching provides clients with structure, support, skills, and strategies."

Most professionals working with adult ADD persons recommend the use of coaches. The person with ADD can realize some of the benefits similar to coaching by joining a focus group. This can also be very helpful because the ADD sufferer will find out that others have the same difficulties they do. They will receive encouragement from others in the group and help from group members sharing their experiences. More information on group formation and existing groups can be found in the appendix.

Chapter 7

Relationship Issues Related to ADD

Relationships are perplexing to many older adults with ADD. Amen (1997) estimates that up to 75% of adults with ADD have interpersonal problems. He gives the following reasons for ADD's interference with the relationship:

** a high rate of intrusive or disruptive behaviors (excessive talking, interrupting, noisy and obnoxious behavior, monopolizing discussions)

** limited social reciprocity (problems taking turns and sharing, difficulty following others in conversations, poor eye contact, inappropriate verbal interchanges)

** poor emotional control (excitability, moodiness, temper outbursts, overreaction to minor events)

** impulsivity (saying or doing things that are thoughtless)

** distractibility (trouble focusing on others)

** lack of follow through (makes relationships feel one-sided from the other person's point of view).

Partners of adults with ADD complain that, "He or she never remembers outings," "won't follow through on projects," "doesn't listen to what I have to say," etc. Many ADD adults resort to drugs and alcohol in an attempt to "slow down" enough to interact with others. Researchers have reported that adults with ADD are more likely to be divorced than adults without ADD (Searight, 1999).

"It's the ADD zone, where what I see is not what's really happening. I feel like people around me are laughing and I've missed the joke. It's like the world is based on some secret code that I can't decipher. I'm always on the brink of making sense out of things, but then I lose it again" (Ratey, Hallowell, & Miller, 1995). This illustrates why adults with ADD have trouble with social relationships. Researchers are beginning to understand how the phenomenology of ADD in adults undermines interpersonal relationships and emotional functioning (Ratey, Hallowell, & Miller 1995, and Ratey & Hallowell, 1994).

Because ADD has only recently been considered an adult disorder as well as a childhood disorder, the specific symptoms and needs of adults with ADD have not yet been fully addressed (Ratey, Hallowell, & Miller, 1995). Quality of life issues, such as relationships, have yet to be studied. There have been several studies of medications for the adult ADD population and treatment modalities have only recently drawn research attention (Barkley, 1990). Most of the information available is based on clinical observation and practice.

The etiology of ADD relationship problems has been attributed to the frontal lobe disinhibition (Chelune, Ferguson, Koon & Dickey, 1986; Douglas, 1984; Gualtieri, Ondrusek & Finely, 1985). The frontal lobes are not functioning properly inhibiting inappropriate responses and integrating moment-by-moment experience with previous experience. Thus the ability to appropriately process information, inhibit responses, anticipate events and modulate emotional reactions is greatly reduced in adults with ADD.

The physiological, behavioral, cognitive, and affective characteristics of ADD act as barriers to forming healthy interpersonal relationships. Intimate interpersonal relationships require a high level of emotional maturity and rely on integration of affective, cognitive, and temporal information. Behaviorally, ADD leads to interrupting the other person or leaving the room in the middle of their conversation, forgetting appointments and plans, being late, having angry outbursts, and having emotional highs and lows. Making relationships even more difficult for individuals with ADD is frequent coexisting personality disorder, which has a possible rate of 25% with ADD (Mannuzza, Klein, Bessler, Mallory, and LaPadula, 1993).

In spite of these negative aspects of ADD, there are many characteristics, which attract non-ADD partners such as spontaneity, creativity and excitement about new experiences. The adult with ADD is attracted to the patience, endurance, and goal-directed focus in a non-ADD person. These differences may first attract, then over time, cause extreme conflict. Once a relationship is formed, forgetting special occasions, making major decisions without the partner's knowing about it, being frequently late or missing appointments and angry out bursts can be very damaging.

The distractibility and focusing problems of ADD may cause distancing from partners, children and grandchildren. Intense, brief, angry outbursts can be very frightening to children (Searight, 1999). Loud outbursts when something goes wrong or becomes frustrating may cause others to become anxious and confused. This behavior may seem to be directed toward the people around them though the person with ADD did not intend it and was unaware of the hurt caused to those with whom he or she has a relationship.

Intimacy is very difficult for those who have ADD. Partners feel they are not able to express their desires, goals, and hurt feelings because the partner with ADD never listens and interrupts frequently. Adults with ADD may be easily drawn to the novelty of a new person, posing a threat to their ultimate relationship. Even when the person with ADD seems to be figuring out what is happening, he or she many times becomes distracted and loses contact. The intricacies of social behavior and nuances of social relationships are difficult for them to recognize and to understand.

Adults with ADD generally have amplified temperamental dispositions, which results in a number of personal and interpersonal problems. The shy person becomes an avoidant person, a loner, and sometimes obsessive-compulsive. The sedate, low-key temperament person becomes clinically depressed. These emotional problems build upon the ADD issues. This may explain the high rates of depression, anxiety, and other co- morbid behaviors for many adults with ADD. Many adults who have compounded disabilities suffer from feelings of shame, humiliation, and inferiority (Ratey, Hallowell, & Miller, 1995). These conditions interfere with the non-ADD partner's ability to communicate his or her needs to the ADD partner who otherwise has no idea what the other person's needs are. The adult with ADD may need to be confronted with his or her defenses and maladaptive coping strategies that have been used to survive but are harmful to partners and to other relationships (Ratey, Hallowell, & Miller, 1995).

Adults with ADD often feel alone even in a relationship. They feel emptiness and do not know how to fill it. Stimulated by social contact, but unable to develop intimacy, they can have a lot of acquaintances but not one with whom they feel close. They feel lonely in a room full of people (Searight, 1999).

The behavioral characteristics of ADD compromise the sincere efforts to establish and maintain intimacy (Ratey, Hallowell, & Miller, 1995). Once the "newness" wears off, the person with ADD gets bored seeks stimulation and looks for new relationships. This has resulted in divorce; however, most adults with ADD work hard to maintain their relationships according to (Ratey & Hallowell, 1994).

Some adults with ADD feel trapped if they are physically close to another adult for an extended period of time (Ratey, Hallowell , Miller, 1995). Those with hyperactivity feel the need to keep moving. Rhythmic touching, such as stroking, can be very annoying to a person having ADD (Weiss, 1997).

There is a strong tendency for a person with ADD to move to the next event, which is not good in close relationships. The disinhibtion, a failure to delay response, causes premature judgments, black and white reasoning, and hasty opinions about people (Nadeau, 1995). Often social cues are misunderstood. Verbal and behavioral expressions are misinterpreted causing inappropriate reactions to the other person's needs, feelings, and desires.

Another emotional barrier common to individuals with ADD is feeling the need to extinguish the existing affect and move to the next. Most adults with ADD want to discharge their emotions and they are not able to postpone discharge to allow the internal processing needed to respond in a socially effective manner to the situation. This prevents them from examining the emotional life of their partner or significant other. Therefore they are unable to develop a sense of empathy (Ratey, Hallowell, & Miller, 1995).

Adults with ADD often experience episodes of stress, dysphoria, and unhappiness, which place significant stress on the relationship. They become emotionally dependent on their non-ADD partners and non-ADD partners may become co-dependent on the ADD partner (Resnick, 2000).

The common complaints from significant others are that their ADD partners (Whiteman, Novotini, 1995):

1. Do not listen
2. Fidget when someone else is talking
3. Try to convince themselves they are in control
4. Let small events cause a deep level of anger
5. Have a poor self-image which results in self blame
6. Do not change things. Some changes are ok such as moving from one task to another. However in a relationship most people with ADD want stability.

Some of the feelings experienced in relationships by adults with ADD are (Sudderth and Kandel, 1997);

1. I'm bored with my husband/wife/girlfriend/boyfriend.
2. They don't understand me.
3. They're always intruding at the wrong time.
4. They make me feel bad when I lose or misplace objects, although invariably I always find them.
5. I'm more comfortable doing things my way than other ways.
6. I don't know why I can't get credit for doing the things I do, rather than for not doing the things that need to get done.
7. I know I'll get to it, if I could just find the time.
8. It's not that I don't want to follow through on things. Rather, it seems like other issues always intrude and more important things come along.

9. It is frustrating when I make lists; I just lose the lists.
10. I'm not comfortable talking about sexual intimacy. I wish there was some way they could understand when I'm "in the mood" and when I'm not.
11. I've never asked him/her to clean up my mess; I like my mess.
12. I really don't try to make my life so hard, it just seems to always happen that way.

Kelly and Novotini, (1993, 1999) outlined these guidelines for practitioners to improve the close relationships of adults with ADD and their partners:

1. Providing a safe environment—help those with AD/HD slow down, focus, become less distracted, and feel safe before beginning to work on relationship issues.

    Guided Imagery
    Relaxation music, ocean waves
    Minimize stimulation and distractions
    Length of time is highly individual, some may need more time, some less
    Structure session, (10 minutes left, and visible clock)
    Teach clients active listening skills including appropriate body language
    Medication usage and timing

2. Help partners understand characteristics of ADD as they relate to intimate relationships.

    Physiological nature of difficulties rather than intentional
    Inattention
    Impulsivity
    Hyperactivity
    Disorganization

3. Help partners develop an awareness of the emotional impact of AD/HD for both the person with ADD as well as the non-ADD partner.

Co-morbidity
The gift of attention
Attribution theory
Over functioning & under functioning

4. Help partners diffuse anger.
   Dialogue
   Emotional reactivity-feeding the anger-
   Anger management tips
5. Identify the strengths that they each bring into the relationship.
   At one time they were connected. What needs to happen to help them reconnect? When the partner focuses on the negatives, they generally lose sight of the positives. What attracted you to him/her? Help them to rediscover things that were meaningful in the partnership. Instill hope.

Educating ADD adults and their partners is helpful. Kelly and Novotini (1993 and 1999):

Top 10 Challenges for those without ADD in relationships with someone with ADD:

1. Emotional reactivity, remain calm
2. Frustration and anger, partner "not getting it"
3. Exhaustion-physical and emotional
4. Lost in partner's problems, not tending to own needs.
5. Confusion-what is and is not ADD?
6. Feeling helpless and overwhelmed.
7. Feeling unappreciated and dismissed
8. Continual struggle to get partner's attention.
9. Being/feeling misunderstood by partner
10. Feeling forced to take control

Top 10 challenges for those with ADD in relationships:

1. Emotional reactivity
2. Being/feeling misunderstood
3. Hypersensivity to tactile stimulation
4. Attentional difficulties-"blinks & blanks"-attention expensive

5. Difficulty with social skills which often limits opportunities for social interaction with others
6. Missing verbal, nonverbal cues and subtext
7. Transitions
8. Easily flooded or overwhelmed
9. Difficulty understanding and reflecting partner's feelings
10. Impatient and easily bored.

What can the person with ADD do to help improve the relationship:

1. Recognize the symptoms associated with ADD and develop efforts to communicate effectively.
2. When the ADD partner is feeling overwhelmed, flooded, confused, angry and/or misunderstood and the non-ADD partner is telling the ADD partner that he or she is "not paying attention." STOP the conversation for at least 20 minutes. Why??? It takes at least 20 minutes for the brain to calm down.
3. Take the 20 minutes to calm down and visualize being in a safe place with no one attacking you or asking questions. Relax, breathe slowly in and out. Allow yourself to drift until you feel calm enough to begin to examine what went wrong.
4. Develop self-awareness. Take a look at this checklist and see if that happened to you:

_____ Was your heart racing?
_____ Were you breathing quickly?
_____ Did you have a knot in your stomach?
_____ Were your thoughts racing?
_____ Were you distracted, restless, tired or bored?
_____ Did you feel confused, anxious, flooded or overwhelmed?
_____ If you are on medication, did you miss a dose?
_____ Were you feeling criticized or attacked?
_____ Were you struggling with information overload?
_____ Were you over-reactive?

____ Were you having difficulty managing your impulses?
____ Were you having difficulty managing your anger?

5. Proceed with caution but with a game plan. You are ready to move back into the conversation when you are calm, focused and understand the difficulties you had in the prior conversation. It is crucial to help your partner understand the difficulties that you are encountering so that you can work together to communicate more effectively.
6. Green light is flashing!!! Now it's time to try again. You are ready and equipped to offer your gift of attention to your partner. Feeling calm and focused you may now return to the discussion with your partner and try out your new game plan.

Other suggestions for people with ADD are (Sudderth and Kandel, 1997):

1. Communication: explain the disorder
2. Take a neutral position.
3. Count to ten before reacting.
4. Organization
5. Determine your role in the relationship
6. Remain an individual
7. ADD is an explanation, not an excuse
8. Negotiate social situations
9. Be nice when you can
10. Use relationship time management

Roberts and Jamsen (1997) in their workbook have a section that is titled "Improve relationships with others by improving knowledge of yourself." They address the following areas:

1. Saying NO, Saying YES, and meaning it
2. Asking for what you want
3. Keeping promises
4. Developing listening skills
5. Interrupting
6. Being blunt
7. Being abrupt
8. Talking too much

9. Committing to a relationship
10. Reading social cues
11. Keeping pace with companions
12. Practicing patience
13. Being honest
14. Showing consideration and compassion for others

The desire to make the relationship work is fundamental to its success. The most important skill for a successful relationship is communication. A critical issue for the counselor helping partners with relationship problems is to train them in blame avoidance. The use of "I" statements rather than "you" statements will help to reduce defensiveness. "You" statements come across as accusing. Also "mind reading" should be avoided since it causes resentment and automatic reactions. Accusing statements should be avoided, "You never remember dates." These labels tend to be repeated and develop a degree of permanence. It is important to remember the older adult with ADD has had a long history of negative labels.

A skill that is very helpful is conflict containment, with methods such as the "time out." This "cool down" before discussing a serious problem helps to avoid conflict. It should not be used to avoid discussion.

Although very difficult for the person with ADD, it is important that the distressed person be able to speak openly without interruption. Also, the distressed individual needs to know they have been heard.

The elements that are important to successful communication between partners are (Kelly and Novotini, 1993, 1999):

1. Mirroring: Reflecting back the content of the message to the person from whom the message came. Paraphrasing is the most common method used.
2. Validation: An indication that the information makes sense.
3. Empathy: Letting the sending partner know that the feelings and images have been received and

emotions that have been sent are recognized and
emotions that have been sent are recognized and
experienced at some level by the receiver.

Some steps to follow that will help with the communication connection.

1. Set a time
2. Find a quiet spot
3. Agree to taking turns
4. Take one issue at a time
5. Don't bring up the past

Techniques used to enhance communication.

1. Angry outbursts – stop communication
2. Emotional flooding – take a time out
3. Interrupting – stop and agree to take turns
4. "You" statements – use "I" statements
5. Automatic negative thoughts – focus on positive aspects.
6. Hypersensitivity – communicate what is happening
7. Impulsivity – stop and think before acting

Older adults with ADD have the problems of younger adults in addition to some problems unique to their age group. These have been discussed in earlier chapters, but they bear repeating. They include medical problems, dementia, age-related depression, isolation and sometimes confinement to a health care facility. These conditions combined with the symptoms of ADD complicate the relationship and the family issues which come with increasing age.

Summary and Conclusions

Since the older adult population is increasing rapidly in comparison to the birthrate, this population is becoming an expanding share of mental health practitioners' caseload. The need for counselors who are able to recognize, diagnose and treat older adults with ADD will grow as more information from research becomes available and the general public becomes more aware that ADD does exist in the older adult population.

ADD can cause devastating problems for people and their partners, family, and friends. If the disorder is recognized and treated properly, it can be successfully managed. First, the person has to know he or she has the disorder and know what it is, and then something can be done about it.

It is vitally important for mental health practitioners to become educated about the disorder and to understand how to differentiate it from other difficulties which older adults experience. Like depression in older adults, ADD also is often mistaken for or attributed to increasing age. This is a disorder that must be recognized by the clinician. Older adults are very unlikely to seek treatment for ADD, having already lived with it all their lives without knowing what it is, that it is a disorder, and that it is treatable.

Because of the prevalence and significant life effects of ADD in older adults, part of every assessment and consultation should include a standard ADD inquiry just as one inquires about alcohol and substance use. Geriatric specialists particularly need to educate themselves for the assessment and diagnosis of older adult ADD.

Older adults with common disorders such as depression, dysthymia, anxiety, substance abuse, learning disorders and bipolar disorders should be evaluated for the possibility of having ADD or being co-morbid with ADD. The appearance of a personality disorder such as narcissistic, borderline, antisocial or paranoid, in older adults may, with early history taking and further assessment, actually be a treatable ADD disorder.

Treatment modalities for older adult ADD are very similar to those used for younger adults and children medication, psychotherapy and education. However, the developmental and life stage issues are different. These interventions are long term and will require frequent fine-tuning as the older adult goes through life cycle changes.

Adults with ADD will need a coach to help them stay with their treatment goals when they face stressful events during the aging process such as a partner's death, retirement, loss of income, or a move to assisted living.

The clinician will find it very gratifying and rewarding to work with older adults who have ADD. Those who receive help will find the quality of their lives so greatly improved that they and others close to them will show extreme gratitude for the help they receive from their health caregivers.

References

Amen, D. G. (1997). Windows into the A.D.D. mind: Understanding and treating attention deficit disorders in the everyday lives of children, adolescents and adults. Fairfield, CA: Mindworks Press.

American Psychiatric Association (1994). Diagnostic and statistical manual of mental disorders, (4th ed.) Washington, DC: American Psychiatric Association.

Barkley, R.A., Fischer, M., Edelbrock, C.S., and Smallish, L. (1990). The adolescent_outcome of hyperactive children diagnosed by research criteria: An 8-year follow up study. Journal of the American Academy of Child and Adolescent Psychiatry, 29, 546-557.

Barkley, R.A. (1990). Primary symptoms and conceptualization in attention deficit hyperactivity disorders: A handbook for diagnoses and treatment. New York: Guilford Press.

Barkley, R.A. (October, 1997). Attention-deficit/hyperactivity disorder. Journal of the American Academy of Child and Adolescent Psychiatry, 36, 1-68.

Beck, A.T., Ward, C.H., Mendelson, M., Mock, J. and Erbaugh, J. (1961). An inventory for measuring depression, Archives of General Psychiatry, 4, 561-571.

Beck, J. S. (1995). Cognitive therapy: Basics and beyond. New York: Guilford Press.

Biederman, J. (1998). A 55-year-old man with attention-deficit/hyperactivity disorder. The Journal of the American Medical Association, 2, 1086-1100.

Biederman, J., Newcorn, J. and Sprich, S. (1991). Comorbidity of attention deficit_hyperactivity disorder with conduct, depressive, anxiety, and other disorders. American Journal of Psychiatry 148: 564-577.

Biederman, J., Faraone, S., Milberger, S. et al., (1996). Predictors of persistence and_remission of ADHD: results from a four-year prospective follow-up study of ADHD children. J Am Acad Child Adolesc Psychiatry 35: 343-351.

Biederman, J., Faraone, S.V., Spencer, T., Wilens, T., Mick, E., and Lapey, K.A. (1994). Gender differences in a sample of adults with attention deficit hyperactivity_disorder. Psychiatry Research, 53, 13-29.

Biederman, J., Faraone, S.V., Spencer, T. et al. (1993). Patterns of psychiatric co-morbidity, cognition and psychosocial functioning in adults with attention deficit_hyperactivity disorder. American Journal of Psychiatry 150: 1792-1798.

Biggs, S.H. (1995). **Neuropsychological and psychoeducational testing in the evaluation of the ADD adult**. In K. Nadeau (Ed.). A comprehensive guide to attention deficit disorder in adults: Research, diagnosis, and treatment (pp. 109-131). New York: Brunner/Mazel.

Breggin, P. (1998). Talking back to ritalin: What doctors aren't telling you about stimulants for children. Monroe, ME: Courage Press.

Brown, T.E., & Gammon, G.D. (1991). The Brown Attention-Activation Disorder Scale: Protocol for clinical use. New Haven, CT: Yale University Press.

Brunk, Doug (2000, February 15). Federal report cites, ADHD diagnosis barriers. Family Practice News, 30, 56.

Chelune, G.J., Ferguson, W., Koon, R., & Dickey, T.O. (1986). **Frontal lobe disinhibition in attention deficit disorder**. In K. Nadeau (Ed.) A comprehensive guide to attention deficit disorder in adults:Research, diagnosis, treatment, (pp. 218-235). New York: Brunner/Mazel.

Copeland, E.D. (1989). Copeland Symptom Checklist for adult attention deficit disorders. Atlanta, GA: Southeastern Psychological Institute.

Douglas, V.I. (1984). **The psychological processes implicated in ADD**. In K. Nadeau (Ed.). A comprehensive guide to attention deficit disorder in adults:Research, diagnosis, treatment, (pp. 221-235). New York: Brunner/Mazel.

DuPaul, G.J., & Stoner, G. (1994). ADHD in the schools: Assessment and intervention strategies. New York: Guilford Press.

Espino, D. V., Jules-Bradley, A., C.O., Johnston, C. L., Mouton, C. P. (2000, March 15). Diagnostic approach to the confused elderly patient. [Online]. American Family Physician. Available: www.aafp.org/afp/980315ap/espino.html

Folstein, M.F., Folstein, S.E., & McHugh, P.R. (1975). Mini-Mental-State, A practical method for grading the cognitive state of the patient for the clinician. Journal of Psychiatric Research, 12, 189-198.

Gerring, J.P., Brady, K. P., Chen, A., Quinn, C., Herskovits, E., Bandeen-Roche, K., Denekla, M., B., Bryan, R.N. (2000). Neuroimaging variables related to development of Secondary Attention Deficit Hyperactivity Disorder after closed head injury in children and adolescents, Brain Injury 14 (3) 205-218.

Goldman, L. S., Genel, M., Bezman, R., J., Slanetz, P.J. (1998). Diagnosis and treatment of attention-deficit/hyperactivity disorder in children and adolescents. The Journal of the American Medical Association, 2 (14), 1100-1108.

Greenhill, L.L., Halperin, J.M., Abckoff, H. (1999). Stimulant Medications, Journal of American Academy of Child and Adolescent Psychiatry, 38: 503-512.

Gualtieri, C.T., Ondrusek, M.G., & Finely, C. (1985). **Attention deficit disorder in adults**. In K. Nadeau (Ed.) A comprehensive guide to attention deficit disorder in adults:Research, diagnosis, treatment (pp. 218-235). New York: Brunner/Mazel.

Guevremont, D.C. (1990). **Social skills and peer relationship training.** In R.A. Barkley (Ed.), Attention deficit hyperactivity disorder: A handbook for diagnosis and treatment (pp. 540-572) New York: Guilford Press.

Hallowell, E.M. & Ratey, J.J. (1994). Driven to distraction: Recognizing and coping with attention deficit disorder from childhood through adulthood. New York: Simon and Schuster.

Herrero, M.E., Hechtman, L. and Weiss, G. (1994). Antisocial disorders in hyperactive subjects from childhood to adulthood: Predictive factors and characteristics of subgroups. American Journal of Orthopsychiatry, 64, 510-521.

Hill, J.C., Schoener, E.P. (1996). Age dependent decline of attention deficit hyperactive disorder. American Journal of Psychiatry, 153, 1143-1146.

Hooberman, D., and Stern, T.A. (1984). Treatment of attention deficit and borderline personality disorders with psychostimulants, case report. Journal of Clinical Psychiatry, 45 (10), 441-442.

Jackson, B. and Farrugia, D. (1997). Diagnosis and treatment of acults with attention deficit hyperactivity disorder, Journal of Counseling and Development, 75, 312-319.

Jasper, L. & Goldberg, I. (1993). Adult ADD questionnaire. [Online]. Mental Health Net. Available: www.MentalHealthNet.com/Adult ADD Questionnaire

Kahn, C.A., Mikalac, C., Benjamin, S., Barkley (1990). **Assessment and treatment of adults with ADHD** In R.A. Barkley (Ed.) Attention deficit hyperactivity disorder: A handbook for diagnosis and treatment. (pp. 613-654). New York: Guilford Press.

Kelly, K.D. (1999, October). Restore the connection in an ADD relationship. Paper presented at the meeting of CHADD (Children and Adults with Attention-Deficit/Hyperactivity Disorder), Washington, D.C.

Kelly, K.D. & Luquet, M.A. (1998). **The impact of adult ADD on couples**. In Loquet, W. & Hannah, M. (Eds.) Healing in the relational paradigm, Washington, D.C: Taylor & Francis.

Kelly, K.D., & Novotni, M. (1999). **The impact of adult ADHD on intimate relationships.** CHADD, We the People: Building Partnerships Through Education, Advocacy, Support and Research, 11th Annual CHADD International Conference, (pp. 281-284). Washington, D.C

Khouzam, H.R. (1997). Attention Deficit Hyperactivity Disorder in Adults: Guidelines for evaluation and treatment, Consultant, 37(8) 2159-2165.

Lavenstein, B. (1995). **Neurological comorbidity patterns/differential diagnosis in adult attention deficit dis-**

order. In K. Nadeau (Ed.) A comprehensive guide to attention deficit disorder in adults;Research, diagnosis, treatment, (pp. 74-92). New York: Brunner/Mazel.

Leimkuhler, E.M. (1995). **Attention deficit disorders in adults and adolescents: Cognitive behavioral and personality styles**. In J.M. Ellison, C.S. Weinstein, and T. Hodel-Malinofsky (Eds.) The psychotherapist's guide to neuropsychiatry: Diagnostic and treatment issues (pp. 174-216) Washington, D.C: American Psychiatric Press.

Lisi, D. M. (2000). Definition of Drug-Induced Cognitive Impairment in the Elderly. [Online]. Medscape Pharmacotherapy. Available: www.medscape.com/Medsape/pharmacology/journal/2000/v02…./pnt-mp0614.lisi.htm

Little, Andrea, Board of Directors of ADDA, (2000). Guiding principles for the diagnosis and treatment of attention deficit hyperactivity disorder. [Online]. The National Attention Deficit Disorder Association. Available: http://www.add.org/gp98.htm

Mahelick, D.M., Carnel, P.W., Greenberg, J.P., Molopskey, W., Brown, T.A., Neary, R.F., Marks, D., Zampella, E., Hodash, R., and Von der Schmidt, I.V. (1998). Psychpharmocologic treatment of acquired attention disorders in children with brain_injury, Pediatric Neurosurgery, 29 (3), 121-126.

Mannuzza, S., Klein, R.G., Bessler, A., Malloy, P., and LaPadula, M. (1993). Adult outcome of hyperactive boys: Educational achievement, occupational rank, and psychiatric status. Archives of General Psychiatry, 50, 565-576.

Merck Manual of Geriatrics (2000). Normal changes of aging and patterns of psychiatric disease. Whitehouse Station, NJ: Merck.

Millon, T. (1981). Disorders of personality:DSM-III, Axis II. NY: Wiley

Nadeau, K.G.(1991). Adult ADHD questionnaire. Annandale, VA: Chesapeake Psychological Services.

Nadeau, K.G. (1995). A comprehensive guide to attention deficit disorder in adults: Research, diagnosis, treatment. New York: Brunner/Mazel.

Nadeau, K. (1995). Life management skills for the adult with ADD, In K. Nadeau (Ed.) A comprehensive guide to attention deficit disorder in adults: Research, diagnosis, treatment. (pp. 191-217). New York: Brunner/Mazel.

Nathan, P.E., Groman, J.M., Salkind, N.S. (1999). Treating mental disorders. New York: Oxford University Press.

National Institute of Health (1998). Diagnosis and treatment of attention deficit hyperactivity disorder (ADHD). N I H Consensus Statement, 16 (2), 1-37.

Neuwirth, S. (1999). National Institute of Mental Health: Attention deficit hyperactivity disorder, (NIMH Publication No. 96-3572). Washington, D.C.: U.S. Government Printing Office.

Novotni, M. (1999). What does everybody else know that I don't?: Social Skills Help for Adults with Attention Deficit Hyperactivity Disorder – A Reader Friendly Guide. Plantation, FL: Specialty Press.

Oeumette, P.C., Brown, P.T. and Najavits, L.M. (1998). Cause and treatment of patients with both substance use and post traumatic stress disorder, Addictions 785-795.

Pardo, J.V., Fox, P.T., and Raichle, M.E. (1991). Localization of a human system for sustained attention by position emission tomography. Nature, 349, 61-64.

Parente, R., and Anderson-Parente, J. (1991). Retraining memory-techniques and applications, Houston, TX: CS4 Publishing.

Practice parameters for the assessment and treatment of children, adolescents, and adults with attention-deficit/hyperactivity disorder, Journal of the American Academy of Child and Adolescent Psychiatry (1997) 36 (10) (Suppl.)

Prochaska, J.O., Norcross, J.C. and DiClemsute, C.C.(1994). Changing for good, New York: William Morrow.

Quinn, P.O. (1995). **Neurobiology of attention deficit disorder**. In K.Nadeau, (Ed.) A comprehensive guide to attention deficit disorder in adults: Research, diagnosis, treatment, (pp. 18-31). New York: Brunner/Mazel.

Ratey, J., Greenberg, S., Bemporad, J.R., & Lindem, K. (1992). **Special diagnostic and treatment considerations in women with attention deficit disorder**. In K. Nadeau (Ed.), A comprehensive guide to attention deficit disorder in adults/Research, diagnosis, treatment (pp. 260-282). New York: Brunner/Mazel.

Ratey, J.J., Hallowell, E.M., & Miller, A.C. (1995). **Relationship dilemmas for adults with ADD:** The biology of intimacy. In K.G. Nadeau (Ed.), A comprehensive guide to attention-deficit disorder in adults: research, diagnosis, treatment (pp. 218-235). New York: Brunner/Mazel.

Resnick, R.J. (2000). The hidden disorder: a clinicians guide to attention deficit hyperactivity disorders in adults, Washington, D.C.: American Psychological Association.

Richardson, W. (1999). The link between ADHD and addiction, Professional Counselor, 30-32.

Roberts, S. M., Jamsen, G. J., (1997). Living with ADD; a workbook for adults with attention deficit disorder. Oakland, CA: New Harbinger Pub.

Roy-Byrne, P., Scheele, L., Brinkley, J., Ward, N., Wiatrak, C., Russo, J., Townes, B. & Varley, C. (1997). Adult attention-deficit hyperactivity disorder: Assessment guideline based on clinical presentation to a specialty clinic, Comprehensive Psychiatry, 38 (3), 33-140.

Sandson, T.T., Bachna, K.J., and Morin, M. D. (2000). Learning disabilities – Physiological aspects attention-deficit hyperactivity disorder – Physiological Aspects, Journal of Learning Disabilities. 33, 83.

Schreiber, H.H., Javorsky, D.J., Robinson, J.E., Stern, R.A. (1999). Reg-Osterrieth complex figure performance in adults with attention deficit hyperactivity disorder: a validation study of the Boston Qualitative scoring system. Clin Neuropsychol 13 (4): 509-520.

Scogin, F. and Prohaska, M. (1993). Aiding older adults with memory complaints. Sarasota, FL: Practitioner's Resource Press, Sarasota.

Searight, R. H., (1999). Close relationships, intimacy, and ADHD. Landover, MD: Attention.

Seligman, M.E.P., (1990). Learned optimism, New York, NY, A.A. Knopf.

Seligman, M.P., (1995). The optimistic child, New York, NY, Houghton Miffin

Semund-Clikeman, M., and Wical, B. (1999). Components of attention in children with complex partial seizures with and without ADHD, Epilepsia. 40(2), 211-215.

Shaywitz, S.E., Fletcher, J.M., Shaywitz, S.E. (1995). Defining and classifying learning disabilities and attention deficit disorder. J. Child Neurol. 10 (Suppl 1), 550-557

Shaywitz, S.E., Fletcher, J.M., Shaywitz, S.E. (1997). Attention-deficit/hyperactivity disorder, Adv Pediatr: 44, 331-367.

Shekim, W.O., Asarnow, R.F., Hess, E., Zaucha, K., and Wheeler, N. (1990). A clinical and demographic profile of a sample of adults with attention deficit disorder, residual state, Comprehensive Psychiatry, 31 (5) 416-425.

Shinka, J. A. (1983). Neuropnysiological Status Examination, Odessa, FL: Psychological Assessment Resources.

Sohlberg, M.M. and Mateer, C.A. (1989). Introduction to cognitive rehabilitation, New York: Guilford Press.

Solden, S. (1995). Women with attention deficit disorder: embracing disorganization at home and in the workplace. Grass Valley, CA: Underwood Books.

Spencer, T., Biederman, J., Wilens, T., et al. (1999). Pharmacotherapy of attention-deficit hyperactivity disorder across the life cycle. Journal American Academy of Child and Adolescent Psychiatry 35: 409-432.

Sudderth, D.B. and Kandel, J. (1997). Adult ADD: The complete handbook, Rocklin, CA: Prima Health Publishing.

Tzelefis, A., Scheikiner, H., & Warbasse, L.H. III, **Differential diagnosis and psychiatric co-morbidity patterns in adult attention deficit disorder**, In K. Nadeau (Ed.) A comprehensive guide to attention deficit disorder in adults: Research, diagnosis, treatment (pp. 35-57). New York: Brunner/Mazel.

Wechsler, D.A. (1987). Memory Scale-Revised Manual. San Diego, CA: The Psychological Corporation.

Weinstein, D., Staffelback, D., Biaggio, M. Attention-deficit hyperactivity disorder and posttraumatic stress disorder: differential diagnosis in childhood sexual abuse, Clin Psycho Rev. 359-378.

Weiss, L. (1997). Attention deficit disorders in adults: Practical help and understanding, Dallas, TX: Taylor Publishing Co.

Weiss, G., and Hechtman, L.T. (1993). Hyperactive children grown up: ADHD in children, adolescents and adults. London: Guilford Press.

Wells, R.D., Dahl, B.B., Snyder, D. (2000). Coping and compensatory strategies used by adults with attention problems, Landover, MD: Attention,.

Wender, P.H. (1987). The hyperactive child, adolescent, and adult: Attention deficit disorder through the life span, New York: Oxford University Press.

Whiteman, T.A., Novotini, M. (1995). **Adult ADD**, In D.B. Sudderth & J. Kandel (Ed.) Adult ADD: The complete handbook, Rocklin, CA: Prima Health Publishing.

Wilens, T., Biederman, J., Mick, E. (1998). Does ADHD affect the course of substance abuse? The American Journal of Addictions 7, 256-163.

Wilens, T., Spencer, T., & Biederman, J. (1995). **Pharmacotherapy of adult ADHD**, In K. Nadeau (Ed.) A comprehensive guide to attention deficit disorder in adults: Research, diagnosis, treatment, (pp. 168-188). New York: Brunner/Mazel.

Wilens, T., et al. (1997). Attention deficit disorder (ADHD) in association with early-onset substance use disorders. Journal of Nervous and Mental Disorders 185, 475-482.

Williams & Wilkins (1997, October). Practice Parameters for the assessment and treatment of children, adolescents, and adults with attention-deficit/hyperactivity disorder, Journal of the American Academy of Child and Adolescent Psychiatry. 36, 1-68.

Zamethkin, A.J., Nordahl, T.E., Gross, M., King, A.C., Semple, W.E., Rumsey, J., Hamburger, S., & Cohen, R.M. (1990). History and overview of adulthood ADD. In K. Nadeau (Ed.) A comprehensive guide to attention deficit disorder in adults: Research, diagnosis, treatment, (pp. 3-17). New York: Brunner/Mazel.

Appendix

Amen's General Adult ADD Symptom Checklist

Please read this list of behaviors and rate yourself (or the person who has asked you to rate him or her) on each behavior listed. Use the following scale and place the appropriate number next to the item.

0 = never
1 = rarely
2 = occasionally
3 = frequently
4 = very frequently

Past History

____ 1. History of ADD symptoms in childhood, such as distractibility, short attention spans, impulsivity or restlessness

____ 2. History of not living up to potential in school or work (report cards with comments such as "not living up to potential)

____ 3. History of frequent behavior problems in school

____ 4. History of bedwetting past 5 years old

____ 5. Family history of ADD, learning problems, mood disorders or substance abuse problems

Short Attention Span/Distractibility

____ 6. Short attention span, unless very interested in something

____ 7. Easily distracted, tendency to drift away

____ 8. Lacks attention to detail, due to distractibility

____ 9. Trouble listening carefully to directions

____10. Frequently misplace things

____ 11. Skips around while reading, or goes to the end first, trouble staying on track or frequently lost

____ 12. Difficulty learning new games, because it is hard to stay on track during directions

____ 13. Easily distracted during sex, causing frequent breaks or turn-offs during lovemaking

____ 14. Poor listening skills

____ 15. Tendency to be easily bored

Restlessness

____ 16. Restlessness, constant motion, legs moving, fidgetiness

____ 17. Has to be moving in order to think

____ 18. Trouble sitting still, such as trouble sitting in one place for too long, sitting at a desk job for long periods, sitting through a movie

____ 19. An internal sense of anxiety or nervousness

Impulsivity

____ 20. Impulsive, in words and/or actions (such as spending)

____ 21. Say just what comes to mind without considering its impact

____ 22. Trouble going through established channels; trouble following proper procedure, an attitude of "read the directions when all else fails"

____ 23. Impatient, low frustration tolerance

____ 24. A prisoner of the moment

____ 25. Frequent traffic violations

____ 26. Frequent, impulsive job changes

____ 27. Tendency to embarrass others

____ 28. Lying or stealing on impulse

Poor Organization

____ 29. Poor organization and planning, trouble maintaining an organized work/living area

____ 30. Chronically late or chronically in a hurry

____ 31. Often have disorganized piles of paperwork or other materials

____ 32. Easily overwhelmed by tasks of daily living

____ 33. Poor financial management (late bills, check book a mess, spending unnecessary money on late fees)

____ 34. Need for others to organize you

Problems Getting Started and Following Through

____ 35. Chronic procrastination or trouble getting started

____ 36. Starting projects not finished, poor follow through

____ 37. Enthusiastic beginnings, but poor endings

____ 38. Spends excessive time at work because of inefficiencies

____ 39. Inconsistent work performance

Negative Internal Feelings

____ 40. Chronic sense of underachievement, feeling you should be much further along in your live than you are

____ 41. Chronic problems with self-esteem

____ 42. Sense of impending doom

____ 43. Mood swings

____ 44. Negativity

____ 45. Frequent feeling of demoralization or that things won't work out for you

Relational Difficulties

____ 46. Trouble sustaining friendships or intimate relationships, promiscuity

____ 47. Trouble with intimacy

____ 48. Tendency to be immature

____ 49. Self-centered; immature interests

____ 50. Failure to see others' needs or activities as important

____ 51. Lack of talking in a relationship

____ 52. Verbally abusive to others

____ 53. Proneness to hysterical outburst

____ 54. Avoids group activities

____ 55. Trouble with authority

Short Fuse

____ 56. Quick responses to slights that are real or imagined

____ 57. Rage outbursts, short fuse

Search For High Stimulation

____ 58. Frequent search for high stimulation (bungee jumping, gambling, race track, high stress jobs, ER doctors, doing many things at once, etc.)

____ 59. Tendency to seek conflict, be argumentative or to start disagreements for the fun of it

Tendency To Get Stuck (thoughts or behaviors)

____ 60. Tendency to worry needlessly and endlessly

____ 61. Tendency toward addictions (food, alcohol, drugs, work)

Switches Things Around

____ 62. Switches around numbers, letters or words

____ 63. Turns words around in conversations

Writing/Fine Motor Coordination Difficulties

____ 64. Poor writing skills (hard to get information from brain to pen)

____ 65. Poor handwriting, often prints

____ 66. Coordination difficulties

Harder I Try The Worse It Gets

____ 67. Performance becomes worse under pressure

____ 68. Test anxiety, or during tests your mind tends to go blank

____ 69. The harder you try, the worse it gets

____ 70. Work or schoolwork deteriorates under pressure

____ 71. Tendency to turn off or become stuck when asked questions in social situations

____ 72. Falls asleep or becomes tired while reading

Sleep/Wake Difficulties

____ 73. Difficulties falling asleep, may be due to too many thoughts at night

____ 74. Difficulty coming awake (may need coffee or other activity before feeling fully awake)

Low Energy

____ 75. Periods of low energy, especially early in the morning and in the afternoon

____ 76. Frequently feeling tired

Sensitive To Noise or Touch

____ 77. Startles easily

____ 78. Sensitive to touch, clothes, noise and light

Answer Key

Total Score: _____ (more than 20 with a score of three or more indicates a strong tendency toward ADD. Items 1, 6, and 7 are essential to make the diagnosis)

Past History 1-5
Short Attention Span/Distractibility 6-15
Restlessness 16-19
Impulsivity 20-28
Poor Organization 29-34
Problems Getting Started and Following Through 35-39
Negative Internal Feelings 40-45
Relational Difficulties 46-55
Short Fuse 56-57
Search For High Stimulation 58-59
Tendency To Get Stuck (thoughts or behaviors) 60-61
Switches Things Around 62-63
Writing/Fine Motor Coordination Difficulties 64-66
The Harder I Try The Worse It Gets 67-72
Sleep/Wake Difficulties 73-74
Low Energy 75-76
Sensitive To Noise Or Touch 77-78

Amen ADD Subtype Checklist

Please rate the following statements on a scale of 0-4
0 indicates that the statement does not at all apply to you;
1 indicates that it rarely applies to you,
2 indicates that it sometimes applies to you,
3 indicates that it often applies to you, and
4 indicates that it very often applies to you.

___1. Often fails to give close attention to details or makes careless mistakes in schoolwork, work, or other activities

___2. Often has difficulty sustaining attention in tasks or play activities
___3. Often does not seem to listen when spoken to directly
___4. Often does not follow through on instructions and fails to finish schoolwork, chores, or duties in the workplace (not due to oppositional behavior or failure to understand instructions
___5. Often has difficulty organizing tasks and activities
___6. Often avoids, dislikes, or is reluctant to engage in tasks that require sustained mental effort (such as paperwork, schoolwork or homework)
___7. Often loses things necessary for tasks or activities (e.g., toys, school assignments, pencils, books, or tools)
___8. Is often easily distracted by extraneous stimuli
___9. Is often forgetful in daily activities
___10. Often fidgets with hands or feet or squirms in seat
___11. Often leaves seat in classroom or in other situations in which remaining seated is expected
___12. Often runs about or climbs excessively in situations in which it is inappropriate (in adolescents or adults, may be limited to subjective feelings of restlessness)
___13. Often has difficulty playing or engaging in leisure activities quietly
__ 14. Is often "on the go" or often acts as if "driven by a motor"
___ 15. Often talks excessively
___16. Often blurts out answers before questions have been completed
___17. Often has difficulty awaiting turn
___18. Often interrupts or intrudes on others (e.g., butts into conversations or games)
___19. Excessive daydreaming
___21. Often appears to be apathetic or unmotivated
___22. Frequently tired, sluggish or slow moving
___23. Frequently spacey or internally preoccupied
___24. Excessive or senseless worrying

___25. Disorganized or super organized
___26. Oppositional, argumentative
___27. Strong tendency to get locked into negative thoughts, having the same thought over and over
___28. Tendency toward compulsive behavior
___29. Intense dislike for change
___30. Tendency to hold grudges
___31. Trouble shifting attention from subject to subject
___32. Difficulties seeing options in situations
___33. Tendency to hold on to own opinion and not listen to others
___34. Tendency to get locked into a course of action, whether or not it is good for the person
___35. Needing to have things done a certain way or you become very upset
___36. Others complain that you worry too much
___37. Moodiness
___38. Negativity
___39. Low energy
___40. Frequent irritability
___41. Tendency to be socially isolated
___42. Frequent feelings of hopelessness, helplessness or excessive guilt
___43. Lowered interest in things that are usually considered fun
___44. Sleep changes (too much or too little)
___45. Chronic low self-esteem
___46. Short fuse or periods of extreme irritability
___47. Periods of rages with little provocation
___48. Often misinterprets comments as negative when they are not
___49. Irritability tends to build, then explodes, then recedes, often tired after a rage
___50. Periods of spaciness or confusion
___51. Periods of panic and/or fear for no specific reason
___52. Visual changes, such as seeing shadows or objects changing shape

___53. Frequent periods of deja vu (feelings of being somewhere before even though you never have)
___54. Sensitivity or mild paranoia
___55. Headaches or abdominal pain of uncertain origin
___56. History of a head injury or family history of violence or explosiveness
___57. Dark thoughts, may involve suicidal or homicidal thoughts
___58. Periods of forgetfulness or memory problems

Answer Key

I.
1-9, 19-23: Inattention (6 of a score of 3 or 4 is needed to make the diagnosis, more than 4 is suspicious)
II.
10-18: Hyperactivity-Impulsivity (6 of a score of 3 or 4 is needed to make diagnosis, more than 4 is suspicious)
III.
24-36: Over focus Issues (6 of a score of 3 or 4 is needed to make diagnosis, more than 4 suspicious)
IV:
37-45: Limbic/Depressive Issues (5 of a score of 3 or 4 is needed to make diagnosis, more than 3 is suspicious)
V:
46-59 Temporal Lobe Issues (6 of a score of 3 or 4 is needed to make diagnosis, more than 4 is suspicious)

Amen Adult General Symptom Checklist

Please rate yourself on each symptoms listed below on a scale from 0-4.
In rating yourself, please use the following scale:

0	1	2	3	4
Never	Rarely	Occasionally	Frequently	Very Frequently

___ 1. Depressed or sad mood
___ 2. Decreased interest in things that are usually fun, including sex
___ 3. Significant weight gain or loss, or marked appetite changes, increased/decreased
___ 4. Recurrent thoughts of death or suicide
___ 5. Sleep changes, lack of sleep or marked increase in sleep
___ 6. Physically agitated or "slowed down"
___ 7. Low energy or feelings of tiredness
___ 8. Feelings of worthlessness, helplessness, hopelessness or guilt
___ 9. Decreased concentration or memory
___10. Periods of an elevated, high or irritable mood
___11. Periods of a very high self-esteem or grandiose thinking
___12. Periods of decreased need for sleep without feeling tired
___13. More talkative than usual or pressure to keep talking
___14. Racing thoughts or frequent jumping from one subject to another
___15. Easily distracted by irrelevant things
___16. Marked increase in activity level
___17. Excessive involvement in pleasurable activities that have the potential for painful consequences (spending money, sexual indiscretions, gambling, foolish business)
___18. Panic attacks, which are periods of intense, unexpected fear or emotional discomfort (list number per month___)
___19. Periods of trouble breathing of feeling smothered
___20. Periods of feeling dizzy, faint or unsteady on your feet
___21. Periods of heart pounding or rapid heart rate
___22. Periods of trembling or shaking
___23. Periods of sweating
___24. Periods of choking
___25. Periods of nausea or abdominal upset

___26. Feelings of a situation "not being real"
___27. Numbness or tingling sensations
___28. Hot or cold flashes
___29. Periods of chest pain or discomfort
___30. Fear of dying
___31. Fear of going crazy or doing something uncontrolled
___32. Avoiding everyday places for fear of having a panic attack or having to go with others in order to feel comfortable
___33. Excessive fear of being judged or scrutinized by other people, which causes you
___34. Persistent, excessive phobia (heights, closed spaces, specific animals, etc.) please list
___35. Recurrent bothersome thoughts, ideas or images which you try to ignore
___36. Trouble getting "stuck" on certain thoughts, having same thought over and over
___37. Excessive or senseless worrying
___38. Others complain that you worry too much or get "stuck" on the same thoughts
___39. Compulsive behaviors that you must do or you feel very anxious, such as excessive hand washing, checking locks, or counting or spelling
___40. Needing to have things done a certain way or you become very upset
___41. Others complain that you do the same thing over and over to an excessive degree (such as cleaning or checking)
___42. Recurrent and upsetting thoughts of a past traumatic event (molest, accident, fire, etc.), please list

____
___43. Recurrent distressing dreams of a past upsetting event
___44. A sense of reliving a past upsetting event
___45. A sense of panic or fear of events that resemble an upsetting past event
___46. You spend effort avoiding thoughts or feelings associated with a past trauma

___47. Persistent avoidance of activities or situations that cause you to remember a past upsetting event
___48. Inability to recall an important aspect of a past upsetting event
___49. Marked decreased interest in important activities
___50. Feeling detached or distant from others
___51. Feeling numb or restricted in your feelings
___52. Feeling that your future is shortened
___53. Quick startle
___54. Feel like you're always watching for bad things to happen
___55. Marked physical response to events that remind you of a past upsetting event, i.e., sweating when getting in a car if you had been in a car accident
___56. Marked irritability or anger outbursts
___57. Unrealistic or excessive worry in at least a couple areas of you life
___58. Trembling, twitching or feeling shaky
___59. Muscle tension, aches or soreness
___60. Feelings of restlessness
___61. Easily fatigued
___62. Shortness of breath or feeling smothered
___63. Heart pounding or racing
___64. Seating or cold clammy hands
___65. Dry mouth
___66. Dizziness or lightheadedness
___67. Nausea, diarrhea; or other abdominal distress
___68. Hot or cold flashes
___69. Frequent urination
___70. Trouble swallowing or "lump in throat"
___71. Feeling keyed up or on edge
___72. Quick startle response or feeling jumpy
___73. Difficult concentrating or "mind going blank"
___74. Trouble falling or staying asleep
___75. Irritability
___76. Trouble sustaining attention or being easily distracted
___77. Difficulty completing projects
___78. Feeling overwhelmed of the tasks of everyday living

___79. Trouble maintaining an organized work or living area
___80. Inconsistent work performance
___81. Lacks attention to detail
___82. Make decisions impulsively
___83. Difficulties delaying what you want, having to have your needs met immediately
___84. Restless, fidgety
___85. Makes a comment to others without considering their impact
___86. Impatient, easily frustrated
___87. Frequent traffic violations or near accidents
___88. Refusal to maintain body weight above at a level most people consider healthy
___89. Intense fear of gaining weight or becoming fat even though underweight
___90. Feelings of being fat, even though you're underweight
___91. Recurrent episodes of binge eating large amounts of food
___92. A feeling of lack of control over eating behavior
___93. Engage in regular activities to purge binges, such as self-induced vomiting, laxatives, diuretics, strict dieting or strenuous exercise
___94. Persistent over concern with body shape and weight
___95. Involuntary physical movement or vocal tics
___96. Delusional or bizarre thoughts (thoughts you know others would think are false)
___97. Seeing objects, shadows or movements that are not real
___98. Hearing voices or sounds that are not real
___99. Periods of time where your thoughts or speech are not connected or do not make sense to you or others
___100.Social isolation or withdrawal
___101.Severely impaired ability to function at home or a work
___102.Peculiar behaviors
___103.Lack of personal hygiene or grooming

___104.Inappropriate mood for the situation (i.e., laughing at sad events)
___105.Marked lack of initiative
___106.Frequent feelings that someone or something is out to hurt you or discredit you
___107.Periods of extreme irritability, physical or verbal aggression or rage with little provocation
___108.Periods of confusion
___109.Periods of spaciness or missing brief periods of time
___110.Periods of fearfulness for no apparent reason
___111.Periods of de ja vu (the feeling that you've been or experienced something before even though you never have)
___112.Periods of unusual visual (seeing) or auditory (hearing) sensations or illusions
___113.Periods of forgetfulness or memory problems
___114.Do you snore loudly (or do others complain about your snoring)
___115.Have others said you stop breathing when you sleep
___116.Do you feel fatigued or tired during the day
___117.Do you often feel cold when others feel fine or they are warm
___118.Do you often feel warm when others feel fine or they are cold
___119.Do you have problems with brittle or dry hair
___120.Do you have problems with dry skin
___121.Do you have problems with sweating
___122.Do you have problems with chronic anxiety or tension

Amen Adult General Symptom Checklist

Diagnostic Answer Key

Condition/Items/(#Items Scored 3 or 4)

Major Depression/1-9/(at least 5 of a score of 3 or more)
Manic Episode/10 plus 11-17/(at least 3 of a score of 3 or more)
Panic Disorder/18 plus 19-31/(at least 4 of a score of 3 or more during a panic attack)
Agoraphobia with or without panic disorder/32
Social Phobia/33/
Simple Phobias/34/
Obsessive Compulsive Disorder/35-41/
Post Traumatic Stress Disorder
/42-45/(at least 1 of a score of 3 or more)
/46-52/(at least 3 of a score of 3 or more)
/53-57/(at least 2 of a score of 3 or more)
Generalized Anxiety Disorter/57 plus
58-75/(at least 6 of a score of 3 or more)
Adult Attention Deficit Disorder
76-87/(at least 5 of a score of 3 or more)
Anorexia Nevosa/88-89/(at least 3 of a score of 3 or more)
Bulimia Nervosa/91-94/(at least 2 of a score of 3 or more)
Tourette's or other tic disorders/95/
Psychotic Disorders/96-105/
Paranoia/106/
Temporal Lobe Symptoms/107-113/
Sleep Apenea/114-116/
Thyroid Abnormalities/117-122/

Additional scales and checklists:

Jasper and Goldberg (1993) <u>On line adult ADD questionnaire,</u> with a scoring system, for self assessment.

Wender (1987) Wender Utah rating scale, A research rating scale, utilizing cut off scores, that emphasizes hyperactivity.

Hallowell and Ratey (1994), A very detailed symptom checklist, without a scoring system

Barkley (1990), University of Massachusetts Medical Center Protocol-a detailed assessment tool utilizing the Symptom Checklist 90-revised, an ADHD checklist and interview with client and close informant(s).

Nadeau (1991): Adult ADHD Questionnaire has a detailed list of questions in 19 categories, with a scoring system.

Books for Adults With ADD:

Adelman, P., and Wren, C.(1990) Learning Disabilities, Graduate School, and Careers: The Student's Prespective. Lake Forest, Il. Learning Opportunities Program, Barat College.

Barkley, R.A., (1998) Attention deficit/hyperactivity disorder: A handbook for diagnosis and treatment (2nd ed) NY, Guilford Press.

Hallowell, E., and Ratey J., (1994) Driven to Distraction, NY, Pantheon Books.

Hartmann, T., (1993) Attention deficit disorder: A new perception, Lancaster, PA Underwood-Miller.

Jackson, M.T. (1997) The Adult attention deficit disorders intervention manual, Columbia, MO, Hawthorn Education Services.

Kelly, K., and Ramundo, P., (1993) You Mean I'm Not Lazy, Stupid or Crazy?!, Cincinnati OH, Tyrell and Jeremy Press.

Nadeau, Kathleen, G., (1995) (Ed), A Comprehensive Guide to attention deficit disorder in adults: Research, diagnosis, and treatment, NY, Brunney/Mazel.

Novotni, M., (1999) What does everyone else know that I don't? Social skills help for adults with attention deficit hyperactivity disorders, Plantation FL, Specialty Press.

Suddreth, Davis, B., and Kandel, Joseph,(1997) Adult ADD: The complete handbook: Everything you need to know about how to cope and live well with ADD/ADHD, Rocklin. CA, Prima Health.

Weiss, G., and Hechtman, L., (1992) (Ed) Hyperactivity Children Grown Up. (2nd ed), NY, Guilford Press.

Weiss, L., (1992) Attention deficit disorder in adults, NY, Taylor Pub. Co.

Wender, P. The hyperactive child, adolescent, and adult:Attention deficit disorder through the life span, NY, Oxford University Press.

National Organizations and Support Groups

Attention Deficit Disorder Association (ADDA)
P.O. Box 972
Mentor, OH 44061
(800) 487-2282
Coaching (ADDA)

Little, Andrea, (2000) Introduction to ADD Coaching, ADDA

Ratey, Nancy (2000) What is ADD Coaching, ADDA

Ratey, Nancy (1999) Therapy and ADD Coaching: Simularities, differences, and collaboration, ADDA

ADDO Foundation
Station R, Box 223
Toronto, Ontario M46 2S9 Canada
(416) 813-6858

ADDult Informational Exchange Network
Box 1991 Ann Arbor, MI 48106
(734) 426-1659

Attention Deficit Information Network (AD-IN)
475 Hillside Avenue
Needham, MA 02194

Children and Adults with Attention Deficit Disorder (CHADD)
8181 Professional Place, Suite 201
Landover, MD 20785

National Attention Deficit Disorder Association (NADDA)
1788 Second Street. Suite 200
Highland Park, IL 60035
1-800-487-2332

ADDvance
1001 Spring Street, Suite 118
Silver Spring, MD 20910
1-888-238-8588

Internet Services

AOL
Go ADD
Compuserve
Go ADD

Prodigy
Under medical support look for ADD topic